Pet Owner's Guide to
RABBITS

Marianne Mays

HOWELL
BOOK HOUSE

New York

HOWELL BOOK HOUSE
A Prentice Hall Macmillan Company
15 Columbus Circle
New York, NY 10023

MACMILLAN is a registered trademark of Macmillan, Inc.

Library of Congress Cataloging-in-Publication data

pet owner's guide to rabbits / marianne mays

Library of Congress catalogue card number: 94–73813
ISBN 0–87605–995–7

Manufactured in Hong Kong

10 9 8 7 6 5 4 3 2 1

Contents

The rabbit is among the most adaptable of all small animals and makes a wonderful family pet.

About the author

Marianne Mays has kept rabbits for many years, and is an experienced breeder and exhibitor. She has cared for a variety of different breeds, but she has specialised in Cashmere Lops and Polish. Marianne has owned two Silver Star Diploma winners, and has supplied winning stock to breeders in Britain and Scandinavia. She has contributed to numerous specialist magazines on small livestock, and has edited a number of club magazines and journals.

Marianne, a qualified veterinary nurse, was born in Sweden and now lives in England with her husband, Nick, who is a specialist in all areas of keeping small livestock. They have two children, and share their home with a variety of pets, including Golden Retrievers, rabbits and pedigree cats, which they breed and show.

Acknowledgements

Many thanks to Shaun Flannery, Lol Middleton, John Symonds, and my husband, Nick, for the photographs; to Sheridan and Stephanie Smith for being such excellent models; to the Doncaster Excelsior Fur Society for letting us photograph rabbits at one of their shows; to the management and staff of Jolleys Pet Superstore, Doncaster, for allowing their stock to be photographed; and last, but not least, to my good friend Linda Dykes for much advice on rabbits and rabbit-keeping over the years. **Marianne Mays.**

A black tan Polish buck – a Silver Star Diploma winner – owned by Marianne Mays

Chapter One

INTRODUCING THE RABBIT

THE ALL-ROUND ANIMAL
The rabbit is among the most resilient and adaptable of animals, and it has maintained a close relationship with mankind for several centuries. Although largely despised by the farming community as a crop-spoiling pest, the rabbit has proved useful to man as a source of food, for fur, for scientific experimentation and, more recently, as a prized, domesticated pet. The European rabbit, *Orcyctolagus cuniculus*, was originally classified as a member of the rodent species. Now it is placed in the order *Lagomorpha* along with hares and pikas.

Physically, the rabbit is a compact animal, with long ears and large, prominent eyes. It has large, powerful hindlegs, which are longer than its forelegs, and enable it to hop and run at speed. The soles of the rabbit's feet have a covering of fur, which provides a firm grip on all kinds of surfaces. The rabbit has a thick, triple-layered coat of dense fur, generally brownish-grey in the normal wild colour. It has a short, white, upturned tail, resembling a cotton-wool ball.

The rabbit is almost exclusively vegetarian in its diet. Its main food in the wild is grass and vegetables. When green food is scarce in winter, it will eat bark. It also gains extra nutrition through the process of eating its own droppings (see Chapter 4). In their wild state, rabbits burrow complicated tunnel systems in the ground, known as warrens. Many warrens are used and added to by successive generations of rabbits over many years. A well-developed warren will have numerous entrances and exits, sleeping areas and even nursery runs for litters.

HISTORICAL BACKGROUND
Rabbits originated in south-western Europe, on the Iberian (Spanish) peninsula and in north-western Africa. They undoubtedly formed part of the meat diet of ancient man although the species was first "officially" discovered by the Phoenicians, the great seafaring traders of the ancient world, circa 1100 BC. The Phoenicians recognised the meat value of rabbits, and traded the animals with the rest of the known world.

The next major port of call for the rabbit was when it was imported to Italy circa 100 BC. This importation was recorded by the Roman scholar, Varro. The Romans kept rabbits in special enclosures called Leporaria, where they would be on hand to provide a constant source of food for the kitchens. The Romans undoubtedly exported semi-domesticated rabbits to all corners of their great empire. Whether any were introduced into Britain during the Roman occupation is unclear – rabbits were not mentioned in any written records from the period.

The rabbit certainly achieved a high status in Roman eyes, for it was depicted on coins issued during the reign of the Emperor Hadrian in the years 120-130AD. There is some evidence that a special longhaired variety of rabbit was developed by Roman stockmen during this time, named the Angora. The breed had long, fine fur which was spun for wool. Many centuries after the Romans, the Angora breed was re-developed, making it perhaps the oldest breed of domestic rabbit in history.

The Normans were well acquainted with rabbits, and they brought several specimens to the British Isles after their successful conquest in 1066. Rabbits were mentioned many times in writings from the 12th and 13th centuries, although it was clear that rabbits were mainly the food of titled, landed gentry. To this end, rabbits were kept in warrens and enclosures in a semi-captive state, drawn upon for food as required. This practice continued well into the 17th century, although by this time, rabbits were considered fair game by the lower classes and poaching of rabbits from private land was rife.

UNDER SIEGE
When British colonists were expanding their great empire they introduced the rabbit to countries such as the United States of America, Australia and New Zealand. Rabbits had no natural enemies in these countries, and they quickly reproduced in vast quantities, decimating crops and grasslands in their quest for food. Mankind hit back with concentrated culling, but they never managed to eradicate the wild rabbit completely. Nowadays, it is against the law to keep pet rabbits in many American states and in most parts of Australia.

In Britain farmers also suffered great crop losses from rabbits. Shooting and trapping failed to make any significant impression on the numbers of rabbits. Then, in 1954 and 1955, the scientific community came up with a disease called Myxomatosis, which would infect rabbits quickly, debilitating them, and then killing them. The disease was introduced to warrens throughout Britain, Europe and Australia, with devastating results for the wild rabbit populations. Since then the disease has declined in virulence, and rabbit populations have made some recovery. However, the disease continues to break out at regular intervals, reducing the rabbit population to an acceptable level.

DEVELOPMENT OF THE RABBIT FANCY
The first leanings towards rabbits being kept as pets came in the early part of the 19th century. During the 1830s and 1840s, various enthusiasts – mainly farmers and landowners – began to develop specialist breeds of rabbits out of captive stock (which were probably kept originally for food). The first true Fancy breed of domestic rabbit was the English Lop, with its huge ear span. This was followed by a spotted breed, ultimately to become known as the English, and the Angora, with its long fur, was re-developed.

In time, quite a few rabbit clubs were formed, ostensibly as an avenue for rabbit breeders to exhibit their newly developed Fancy specimens in competition. One of the earliest and most influential rabbit clubs was the Metropolitan Rabbit Club, founded circa 1845. In the 1870s, a number of national clubs were formed, each vying to control the growing Rabbit Fancy, as more breeds of Fancy Rabbit were created. None of these early national clubs lasted very long.

By the 1890s, quite a number of specialist breed clubs had been established,

The birth of the Rabbit Fancy saw a huge development in the number of different breeds. This is a Siamese Smoke Netherland Dwarf.

Pictured below is an English Lop, butterfly agouti in colour.

Rabbit-showing is now a popular pastime worldwide.

It is as a family pet that the rabbit reigns supreme.

including the Himalayan, Dutch and English breed clubs. After the First World War, around 1919, Mr P.E. Wilson formed the National Table Rabbit Society, which, as its name suggests, was more geared towards commercial food and fur rabbits. It was the long-established Beveren Club, however, which undertook to provide governing coverage to the various specialist clubs. Initially, the club catered for the Fur breeds of rabbit and changed its name to the British Fur Rabbit Society. Later it changed its name to the British Rabbit Society, in deference to the other breed categories of rabbit, namely Rex and Fancy. In 1928 James Pickard, an eminent scientist and animal fancier, founded the National Rabbit Council of Great Britain and the Dominions. This club was dedicated to scientific and genetic research into the Fur breeds of rabbit.

Both governing bodies existed simultaneously for some time. However, many rabbit fanciers considered that it was a ridiculous situation to have two governing bodies for the same Fancy. A mediator towards uniting both camps came in the form of J.E. Watmough, himself a prominent fancier and then editor of the main fanciers' newspaper, *Fur & Feather*. Watmough suggested an amalgamation in 1932. It took two years to complete but, in 1934, the union was complete and the British Rabbit Council was formed.

The BRC has administered the Rabbit Fancy ever since, overseeing the multitude of regional, local and specialist breed rabbit clubs and societies which exist today. The BRC also controls the registration of Fancy rabbits, the various standards of each breed and variety of rabbit, and the training and registration of rabbit judges. It also allocates the various star ratings to shows. The American Rabbit Breeders Association, based in the USA, fulfils the same function as its UK counterpart, covering all affiliated rabbit clubs spread across the United States.

Chapter Two

ACQUIRING A PET RABBIT

IS A RABBIT A SUITABLE PET?
Whether or not a rabbit will make a suitable pet depends on a lot of factors, such as the age of the intended owner, the breed of the rabbit, and whether the prospective rabbit owner lives in a small apartment, or a house with a yard or a garden. Rabbits can make wonderful pets for young and old alike, but it is important to carefully consider every aspect of rabbit keeping before actually acquiring one.

First of all, who is going to be responsible for the rabbit? A rabbit is a living animal, that will need feeding and care throughout its life, which may be five years or more. It is not a toy to discard when the novelty has worn off. If the rabbit is intended as a pet for a child, it is important to remember that the ultimate responsibility has to lie with an adult. Young children cannot be expected to take full responsibility for an animal, at least not before the age of twelve years.

Rabbits can become very tame and friendly, but they are not an ideal pet for the very young child. A rabbit is not a pet that is content with sitting still on its owner's lap for long periods of time. The rabbit has strong hindlegs which are capable of kicking and hurting a small child who is not yet strong enough to handle the rabbit properly. I would suggest that no child under the age of seven should be given a pet rabbit. If the younger child wants a pet, the more easy-going guinea pig is a very good alternative.

The second important aspect to consider is where the rabbit is going to be housed. Rabbits prefer to live outdoors, so a hutch in the back garden is usually the best alternative. But do not despair if you do not have such facilities, there are other options. Rabbits can be kept in a shed or a garage (but not a garage where a car is kept, as the fuel fumes could be harmful), or even on the balcony of a high-rise apartment. Whenever possible, the rabbit should be kept outdoors. It will be much happier living outside than inside with central heating. A warm environment will bother the rabbit much more than a cold one.

However, all is not lost if you live in an apartment which has no garden or balcony. It is quite possible to keep a rabbit indoors – but it will require much work from its owner. An indoor hutch must be cleaned out very regularly in order to prevent bad odours. If the rabbit is let out to exercise, care must be taken to ensure that it does not chew electrical cables or anything else potentially dangerous. Indoor rabbits can become house trained, although it should be borne in mind that not all rabbits will learn this. It is also important to restrict yourself to a small breed if you are keeping your rabbit indoors, as space will be limited.

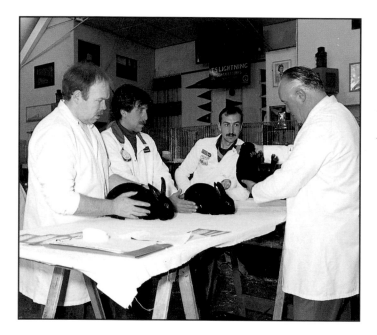

A rabbit show is the best place to go if you want to find out more about rabbit breeds.

The Dwarf Lop is the ideal breed for most people.

The Polish is small and pretty, but its temper makes it unsuitable as a pet, unless you are a very experienced rabbit-keeper.

This broken-marked cross-breed is typical of many pet rabbits. The disadvantage of buying a cross-breed is that you have no indication of what size the rabbit will grow to, or what its temperament will be like.

WHERE TO BUY A RABBIT

Most people will probably visit their local pet shop to buy a pet rabbit. This can work very well, if the pet shop is a good one with knowledgeable staff, and all you want is a nice pet. However, visiting a rabbit breeder does have many advantages. A breeder will be able to sell you a rabbit of the exact breed that you want, whereas supplies in pet shops are often limited, or consist of crossbred rabbits only.

A breeder will also be able to tell you the exact date of birth of your chosen rabbit, what it has been used to eating, and you can probably meet the rabbit's parents so you will have an idea of what your rabbit will be like as an adult. This is important not only as regards size, but you will also be able to judge whether the rabbit is likely to be a good pet or not. If the parents are nice and friendly, the chances are that your rabbit will have a similar temperament. Your local rabbit club will be able to give you details of rabbit breeders in your area.

Unfortunately, unwanted rabbits often end up in animal shelters, and you would be doing a good deed if you decided to take on an adult, unwanted rabbit. The staff at the shelter should be able to tell you a little about the rabbit's background history, and what its temperament is like.

CHOOSING A RABBIT BREED

Rabbits come in many different breeds, and not all will make suitable pets. For example, the popular Dwarf Lop will make an ideal pet for most people, whereas the lively little Polish, although very small and pretty, has got quite a nasty temper and will not make a good pet for anybody except the very experienced rabbit keeper. Crossbred rabbits can make very good pets, but by choosing a crossbreed rather than a pedigree breed, you are rather relying on luck. You will know nothing about what size the rabbit will eventually grow to, and what sort of temperament it is likely to have. The various breeds of rabbit, and their suitability as pets, will be discussed in Chapter Five.

MALE OR FEMALE?

Generally speaking, bucks (males) will make better pets than does (females). A buck will often be slightly more easy-going and friendly than a doe. An adult doe rabbit, who is not being bred from, will often become almost obsessed with breeding. If not bred from, she may become aggressive, and will often also develop so-called phantom pregnancies – when she believes that she is pregnant, although she is not. A doe will also often be more territorial than a buck, defending her hutch from intruders (which may be the owner!).

A buck rabbit can also become aggressive and defend his territory, and the entire buck may develop the annoying habit of spraying. A spraying buck rabbit will literally spray urine over anything that he considers belongs to him, and that includes his owner! Not all bucks spray, but it is seldom possible to predict which young buck is going to become a sprayer as an adult, and which will not. There is, however, a way to get round most of the problems that may be associated with buck rabbits. If the rabbit is not intended for breeding, a vet can neuter him. This will usually calm the rabbit down considerably, stop him from spraying, and will most often improve a bad temper. Therefore, you are perhaps safer in acquiring a buck rather than a doe, as it is easier to correct any undesirable behaviour. Neutering of does is not normally done, as it is a very major operation for such a small animal.

HOW MANY RABBITS?
Most people tend to think that it is kindest to get two rabbits, so that they can keep each other company. Nothing could be further from the truth. Some rabbits will live happily together, but most will fight. Once adult, rabbits should always be kept singly. Even two rabbits of the same sex, from the same litter, are likely to start fighting eventually, often with disastrous results. Two sisters may live happily together, but a really large hutch with a run is required, and there is no guarantee that they will live together in harmony. Two adult buck rabbits will never live together peaceably, and a buck and a doe is also an impossibility, as the doe will be mated time and time again – and she will probably kill her offspring soon after birth because of the presence of a buck.

If you are absolutely convinced that you want two rabbits living together, then choose the breed with care. Breeds such as the Dwarf Lop and the Cashmere Lop, which are very easy-going breeds, may sometimes live together in peace. Other breeds, such as the Netherland Dwarf and the Polish, will never, ever accept another rabbit in the same hutch.

A very good alternative to keeping two rabbits together, is to keep one rabbit and one guinea pig. These animals will live together happily, and can become good friends. It is preferable to introduce the rabbit and the guinea pig when they are both young, as they may find it hard to accept a companion in later life. Make sure that the rabbit you choose is not of a large breed, as a very large rabbit may kill the much smaller guinea pig by mistake, just by stamping his feet.

SELECTING A HEALTHY RABBIT
Having decided on the breed and sex of rabbit you want, the next step is to choose a rabbit that is fit and healthy. This can be done by running through a simple check list of points to bear in mind:

1. AGE: A rabbit should not be sold under the age of six weeks. Smaller breeds, such as the Netherland Dwarf, can leave their mother for a new home at the age of six weeks, but really large breeds, such as the French Lop, often need a little longer to mature, so they are best left until the age of eight to nine weeks.

2. BEHAVIOUR: The rabbit should be lively and curious. It should not be frightened, and should not appear listless.

3. EARS: The ears should be clean, free from any crustiness inside or outside. A rabbit of any lop breed may not have lopped by six to eight weeks of age, and the youngster may have semi-erect ears. This is normal – the ears should have lopped by the age of twelve weeks.

3. NOSE: The nose should be clean with no discharge, and there must be no evidence of sneezing.

4. TAIL AREA: The tail and surrounding areas should be clean and dry, with no sign of diarrhoea.

If you want to keep more than one rabbit, it is advisable to pick an easy-going breed such as the Cashmere Lop.

A rabbit and a guinea pig will live together quite happily and will become good friends.

Rabbits and dogs do not have to be natural enemies. However, the dog must be well-trained, and you must always supervise sessions when they are together.

This pair may never become the best of friends, but a rabbit who has been carefully trained will learn to adapt to a variety of different experiences.

5. FUR: The fur should be soft and dense, and free from mites or dirt. A longhaired rabbit may have a slightly bald neck as a youngster, as the baby fur does not cover the body as well as the adult fur. This is acceptable, but beware of bald patches over the body. A shorthaired breed must have no bare patches at all.

6. FEET: The rabbit's feet should be clean. It is especially important to check the inside of the front legs. If the fur there is matted, it is a sign that the rabbit has been using its front legs to wipe a runny nose. The claws should be short and sharp; overgrown claws indicate that the rabbit is not a youngster.

7. BODY: The whole body should be firm and even. It must not be too thin, or have an extended pot-belly, as this may indicate the presence of worms or some form of disease.

SEXING RABBITS

It is essential to learn how to sex a rabbit in order to be able to select the sex of your choice. This can be quite a difficult task with young rabbits, so even if you are buying your rabbit from an experienced breeder, it is important to be able to double check. Unlike most animals, rabbits cannot be sexed at birth. It takes at least four or five weeks before it is possible to determine the sex of a baby rabbit. Large breeds are usually slightly easier to sex than smaller ones, simply because their genitalia are larger.

The easiest way of determining the sex of a young rabbit is to place the rabbit on its back on the palm of one of your hands. Make sure that you have a good grip, as small rabbits can jump surprisingly well. With the other hand, gently press with two fingers around the sexual organ. A small opening will then be visible. In the buck rabbit, this will appear in the form of a circle, in the doe the opening will look like a V-shaped slit. If all the youngsters examined appear to have a circular opening, it may be because they are slightly too young to be sexed properly. If this is the case, wait a week and try again. If you still get the same result, then you can safely assume that they are all bucks! It is much easier to sex the adult rabbit. An adult buck will have two fairly large testicles that are clearly visible. The doe's vagina will show as a large V-shaped opening.

Chapter Three

EQUIPMENT

It is a very good idea to purchase all the equipment needed for a pet rabbit before you actually bring your new pet home. A rabbit will need peace and quiet during the first few days in a new home – it needs time to settle down and get used to its new surroundings. This is more easily achieved if everything is ready and waiting for the rabbit on its arrival, with the hutch fully furnished and the appropriate food in stock.

THE CAGE
The single most important piece of equipment that your rabbit will need is a cage to live in. The most common type of cage is the wooden rabbit hutch, although in America all-wire metal cages are often used. Some countries also have specially-built indoor rabbit cages available.
    The type of hutch or cage you purchase for your rabbit depends on two important factors. Firstly, where the hutch is to be situated, and secondly the size of the rabbit that is going to live in it.

THE OUTSIDE HUTCH
A hutch that is going to be located outside must be fully weather-proofed and able to withstand rain, snow and wind, as well as very hot and sunny weather. The outdoor hutch must be made of wood, as either metal or plastic will become far too cold in the winter and hot in summer. The very best type is tongued and grooved, made of heavy wood. A plywood hutch does not offer sufficient protection against really cold weather, and it is less likely to survive for as long as the rabbit! If you intend to keep your rabbit outside, it is advisable to spend a little bit more money on a hutch that will serve you and your rabbit well for several years.
    The outdoor hutch must be treated with wood preserver or it will eventually begin to rot. Some hutches come pre-treated, and this will be made clear by the manufacturer. If you are treating the hutch yourself, you must ensure that the preserver you use is non-toxic to animals. A hutch will usually need a new coat of preserver every few years to keep it in good condition. Remember to treat it on the inside as well as on the outside.
    The best type of outdoor hutch will have a separate sleeping compartment or a partly covered front. This is necessary so that the rabbit can take shelter during bad weather. Approximately one-third of the front of the hutch should be covered, with the rest being made of tough wire. Never use a hutch that has flimsy chicken-wire as a front, as the rabbit needs to be well protected from dangers such as stray cats or dogs.

A good pet store will stock a wide range of rabbit hutches. There will be a variety of sizes to suit the different sizes of rabbit breeds.

An indoor cage, suitable in size for Dwarf rabbits.

A single rabbit hutch suitable for outdoor use. This hutch is slightly raised off the ground and has been treated with a wood preserver. It has a sloping, felted roof.

The separate sleeping compartment is covered to provide maximum warmth and comfort.

The roof of the outside hutch is very important. A flat roof is to be avoided, as rainwater will gather on top. The roof should either be sloping (preferably with a slight overhang over the front) or apex. In this way, no water can gather on top of the hutch. The roof should be covered with roofing felt, as treating it with wood preserver will not be enough to keep it leak-proof.

An outdoor hutch should never be placed directly on the ground; it must always be raised at least a couple of inches (5cms). This will keep the hutch warmer, and it will also make it easier for you to clean out. It will also prevent the base from rotting due to dampness. Some hutches are supplied with short legs, or you can place the hutch on top of something, such as a few bricks, to raise it further off the ground.

An outside hutch should preferably be placed with its back against a house or outbuilding, for maximum protection. Make sure that it is perfectly steady and cannot fall over. In very bad weather the front of the hutch can be covered with tarpaulin or something similar, making sure that the rabbit has got an adequate air supply.

THE INDOOR HUTCH
This can be more simply constructed than an outside hutch. In this instance, plywood will be perfectly suitable, although it is still a good idea to treat it with wood preserver, as this will stop the rabbit's urine from seeping into the wood, and it will prolong the life of the hutch. The front can be all wire, and the roof can be flat. It is preferable to have the hutch slightly raised off the ground, or placed on an old table, as this will enable you to clean it out without having to kneel on the floor. A separate sleeping compartment is not necessary.

THE INDOOR CAGE
An indoor cage should have a plastic bottom tray, with a wire canopy. This type of cage is easy to clean out and keep free of odour.

SPECIAL NEEDS
Angora rabbits need a special type of housing due to their long fur. They need to be kept in a cage or hutch with a wire floor. This is so that the rabbit's droppings and urine can fall through the floor on to a covered tray underneath. An Angora rabbit that is kept in an ordinary hutch will soon become very dirty, and its fur will get tangled and knotty, with wood shavings and hay sticking to it. For the same reason, the hay fed to an Angora should be tied to the side of the cage, or kept in a hayrack.

The Angora has got very heavily-furred feet, so the wire floor will not bother it. However, other breeds are best kept on an ordinary floor, covered with bedding. This applies particularly to the Rex rabbit, which has very short fur on its feet, and would suffer if it was kept on a wire floor. Other Longhair breeds, such as the Cashmere Lop or the Swiss Fox, do not have the same woolly coat as the Angora, so they will not suffer if they are kept like shorthaired rabbits.

RECOMMENDED FEATURES
For the sake of convenience and safety, there are certain features well worth looking out for in the hutch that you intend to buy:

A LITTER BOARD: This is a long piece of wood placed at the front of the rabbit hutch. Ideally it should be removable and should not be attached to the hutch door. The litter board will prevent wood shavings and other bedding from falling out of the hutch, and it will also make the hutch safer for the rabbit, once the door is open. When removed, cleaning out will be made easy.

ANTI-CHEW DEVICES: These are pieces of tough plastic, placed on the inside of the rabbit hutch, to prevent the rabbit from chewing any wood that may be easily accessible.

ACCESS: If the hutch has a separate sleeping compartment, check that the opening between the bedroom and the main hutch is not too small – the rabbit should be able to get in and out easily. Avoid openings that consist of a single round hole; opt for the type that looks more like a traditional door. If the rabbit has to jump through the hole, it may injure itself.

FRONT OPENING: The front opening of the hutch, or the door, should ideally swing either to the right or to the left, or it should be possible to completely remove the front. Doors that swing upwards or downwards are very awkward to keep in place when you are cleaning out.

SIZE: The size of the hutch is obviously very important. The bigger the rabbit, the bigger the hutch – that is common sense. As a general guideline, a hutch for a small or medium-sized breed, such as a Netherland Dwarf or a Dutch, should be no smaller than 24ins by 24ins (60cms by 60cms). For a larger breed, such as a New Zealand, a hutch 36ins by 24ins (90cms by 60cms) will be necessary. The giant breeds, such as the French Lop, will need really large hutches, measuring a minimum of 48ins by 24ins (120cms by 60cms).

HEIGHT: The rabbit must be able to stand up on its hindlegs (something rabbits often do) without touching the roof of the hutch with its head. Once again, the bigger the rabbit, the taller the hutch must be.

FURNISHING THE HUTCH

Once the hutch has been purchased, it needs to be furnished. However, the rabbit's requirements are not very extensive. You will need to buy bedding, a bowl for food, a gravity water bottle, and perhaps a fruit tree branch to chew, and/or a salt licking stone.

BEDDING

The type of bedding you decide to use will depend on whether the rabbit is kept inside or outside, as well as on the time of year. A rabbit kept in the house or in a garden shed, will be happy with a layer of wood shavings and some hay. Never use sawdust, as this is far too fine, and can seriously injure your rabbit by getting into its nostrils and into its eyes. The wood shavings you purchase should be specifically for use with pets, and can be bought from pet shops or wholesalers. This type will be clean and perfectly safe for your pet. If you get your shavings from your local lumberyard, you cannot be entirely sure that the wood turned into shavings has not been treated with any poisonous preservatives.

An outdoor rabbit can have the same bedding as an indoor one during warm weather, but during a cold or rainy winter it will need extra protection. This is best achieved by laying a thick layer of straw on top of the shavings. Remember that rabbits can withstand very cold temperatures – they do, in fact, prefer cold

The Angora needs special care because of its long fur. The cage or hutch must have a wire floor so that droppings and urine can fall through to a covered tray underneath.

Rex rabbits, like this Siamese Sable Rex, have very short fur on their feet and would suffer if kept on a wire floor.

A litter board will prevent bedding and wood shavings from being kicked out of the hutch.

The larger breeds, such as this New Zealand Red, need a hutch that measures a minimum of 36ins by 24ins (90cms by 60cms). A rabbit must have enough room to stand up on its hindlegs without touching the roof with its head.

conditions to warm. However, they cannot withstand a wet or draughty hutch.

Never be tempted to use newspaper as bedding for your rabbit. The rabbit will tear it to pieces, making a very untidy hutch, and the ink can be poisonous. Also, a rabbit of pale coloration will become stained by the ink.

OUTSIDE RUN

Most rabbits will benefit from having an outside run. Some hutches come with a run attached, or a separate run can be purchased from most pet shops. It is also quite possible to make your own run, using wood and tough wire. A run is for placing on the grass, so that the rabbit can enjoy more freedom than usual and can also nibble at the grass. However, this is not appropriate in cold or wet weather, so a hutch with an attached run is not a good idea.

The ideal rabbit run is large enough for the rabbit to move about in – larger than its usual hutch. It must have some sort of a lid, as rabbits can jump very high and so it must be escape-proof. The bottom of the run should be covered with wire, to prevent the rabbit from digging its way out. Ideally, there should be a covered area in the run, where the rabbit can take shelter from hot sun or rain.

BREEDING HUTCH

For the person who owns several rabbits, special breeding hutches can be purchased. These come in blocks of several hutches together, not dissimilar to a block of apartments. It is possible to get a block from as few as two hutch compartments to as many as twenty-four, in varying sizes. Your local rabbit club will probably be able to advise you of your nearest manufacturer of hutches, as this sort is not normally sold in pet shops.

FOOD BOWLS

A good quality food bowl is a must for the rabbit hutch, as many rabbits will not eat food straight off the floor. The food bowl is for the rabbit mix or pellets which will be fed to your rabbit. Any green food that might be fed can be put straight on the floor.

The ideal food bowl is quite heavy, so that the rabbit cannot tip it over. An earthenware bowl is ideal, such as sold for dogs and cats in pet shops. Alternatively, a metal bowl which hooks on to the wire front of the rabbit hutch can be used. There are so-called hoppers on the market, which are placed outside the cage. This type of bowl only really works with an all-wire cage. A plastic bowl of any kind should never be used. The rabbit will soon chew it to pieces, and may become ill if it swallows a piece of plastic.

DRINKING BOTTLES

The best way to provide your rabbit with a good supply of water (something which must always be available) is to fit a gravity water bottle to the front of the hutch. Bottles of many shapes and sizes can be bought in pet shops. The type with a ball point tube is usually the best, as it is less likely to leak than other types. Most rabbits drink quite a fair amount of water, especially if they are not fed green food, so one of the larger sizes of drinking bottle available is recommended. It is not a good idea to use a water bowl rather than a bottle, as the water is easily spilled and it very quickly becomes heavily soiled.

GROOMING EQUIPMENT
There are a few items of grooming equipment you will need to buy in order to keep your rabbit in top-class condition.

NAIL-CLIPPERS
All rabbits will need their claws trimmed from time to time, so a good pair of nail clippers is an essential item of equipment. There are several to choose from. The best type is probably one that is intended for cats – they look like small wire-cutters. Nail clippers for dogs can be used, but they tend to be too big and clumsy for a small rabbit. Your local pet shop should be able to show you a selection of nail-clippers, and give you advice.

COMBS
Any rabbit of a longhaired breed will require regular grooming, and the shorthaired breeds will benefit from some grooming during shedding in order to remove dead hair. The best type of comb is a fine-toothed metal comb, such as the type made for cats. This will remove dead hairs easily from a shorthaired breed, and will put the finishing touches to a well-groomed longhaired breed. For a longhaired breed, a metal comb with wider teeth is also necessary. This will be needed to remove any knots, and to get through slightly matted fur.

SLICKER BRUSH
This is useful for both shorthaired and longhaired breeds. No other type of brush will get through the rabbit's dense fur.

TRAVELLING BOXES
There will always come a time when you need to transport your rabbit for one reason or another, be it to a show or for a visit to the vet. This is when a travelling box is essential. Never attempt to transport a rabbit in a cardboard box, as it is not sufficiently secure. The rabbit can push its way through the lid, or even chew its way out. A proper box is essential.

Rabbit boxes come in many different sizes, and are usually made of wood. They are complete with ventilation holes and a carrying strap. Most rabbit hutch manufacturers will also make travelling boxes. Ask your local rabbit club for details. Unfortunately, rabbit travelling boxes are not available from pet shops.

If you cannot get hold of a proper rabbit travelling box, a plastic cat carrier is a reasonable alternative. The cat carrier or rabbit travelling box will also come in handy when you clean out the rabbit's hutch – it is perfect for putting the rabbit inside while you attend to its housekeeping.

OTHER USEFUL EQUIPMENT
There are items that are not essential for the well-being of your rabbit, but which may, nonetheless, make life a little easier for the owner. These include:

1. A rubber mat: To sit the rabbit on while it is being groomed or examined.
2. A hayrack: To prevent hay from being soiled. This can be bought from well-stocked pet shops, or can be easily constructed out of wire mesh, which is attached to the rabbit's hutch in the shape of a basket.

Rabbit bowls should be either ceramic or made of metal. A gravity water-bottle is the best way to supply your rabbit with fresh clean water.

Grooming equipment (left to right): A slicker pad, a nail-trimmer, and metal combs.

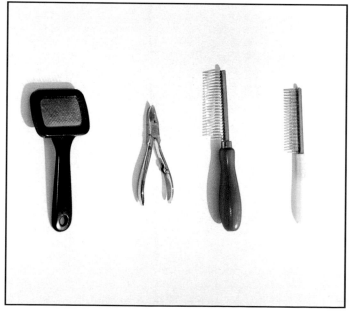

A rabbit travelling box, suitable for transporting your rabbit to the vet or to a show.

Most rabbit boxes have a removable divider, so that either one or two rabbits can travel, as required.

3. A bottle-brush: Preferably of the kind sold for babies' feeding bottles. This will help to keep your rabbit's water-bottle free from algae, which quickly builds up, especially in warm, sunny weather.

4. Plastic water piping: This is for the rabbit kept indoors. It is used to cover any electrical cables or wires, which could be chewed by a rabbit.

5. A cat litter tray: This encourages the rabbit to be clean in the house, even when it is not near its hutch. The tray should be filled with non-clumping cat litter. (Rabbits do not like the sort of litter which clumps, as it sticks to their feet.) Put a few rabbit's droppings in the tray and repeatedly place the rabbit inside it while it is exercising. Hopefully, the rabbit will soon get the idea!

6. Toys: I have found that some rabbits like to play with toys, such as jingling balls, intended for cats. Make sure the toys are made of tough plastic which cannot easily be chewed.

Chapter Four

CARING FOR YOUR RABBIT

FEEDING

The most important aspect of caring for your pet rabbit is providing the correct diet. The rabbit has a very sensitive digestive system, and it is vital to ensure that every rabbit is fed according to age, size, breed, and whether it is being kept in a cold or hot environment.

The first important rule is never attempt to change the rabbit's diet from one day to another. A drastic change in diet can cause serious stomach upsets, and in extreme cases it could result in the death of the rabbit. Some rabbits are naturally less sensitive than others, but you should always treat each rabbit as if it were very sensitive, just to be on the safe side.

SETTLING IN

When you collect your new rabbit, be it from the pet shop or the breeder, you must find out what the rabbit has been fed on. It is important to feed it on the same food for at least a few days. If you want to feed your rabbit differently, the change from one diet to another must be done gradually. Start by feeding the rabbit the same food that it has been used to for two to three days. After this, you can gradually start to mix in small quantities of the new food with the old diet, in the proportions of one quarter of new food to three-quarters of old food. Continue feeding this mixture for a few days, and carefully observe the rabbit to see if the diet change has caused any problems, such as diarrhoea. If all is well, you can increase the amount of new food, until eventually your rabbit is eating its new diet exclusively.

DIETARY REQUIREMENTS

There are numerous different kinds of rabbit feeds on the market, and it can be quite a task to select the best one. Almost all rabbit foods are 'complete', that is, a food that includes all the necessary nutrients and vitamins for a rabbit. However, you must make sure that the food contains the right amount of protein for your rabbit. The average pet rabbit will need 12 to 14 per cent of protein. If the diet contains any more than this the rabbit will quickly become overweight and may develop all sorts of problems, such as a fatty liver or kidney failure.

However, a rabbit that is used for breeding, especially the pregnant and nursing doe, will need a higher amount of protein in her food to help her cope. A ratio of 16-18 per cent of protein is usually appropriate. Likewise, rabbits kept in very cold weather will benefit from a higher protein level, as this helps them to keep warm. In cold weather the amount fed to the rabbit will also have to be increased. Young

A good, balanced diet is essential for your rabbit's health and well-being. The main part of the diet should consist of a dry mix of pellets, flaked maize, crushed peas, oats and wheat.

Water must be changed regularly, particularly in hot weather.

Beware of introducing green food to the diet, as rabbits have very delicate stomachs.

*Most rabbits
are quite
happy if they
are fed once a
day*

rabbits of large breeds, such as French Lops, will also benefit from higher protein levels until they are fully grown, when the usual 12-14 per cent can be fed.

A rabbit should always be fed on a food specially prepared for rabbits. Do not be tempted to feed it anything intended for other animals, such as hamsters, guinea pigs or even goats and ponies. These animals will invariably have different dietary needs to the rabbit, and the foods will contain too high a level of protein. In the case of hamster mixes, these often contain sunflower seeds and peanuts, which should not be fed to rabbits as they are too fattening, and could also become a hazard by sticking to the rabbit's teeth.

PELLETS AND MIXES

If your rabbit was purchased from a breeder, the best bet is to continue to feed what the breeder recommends. Most breeders will have many years' experience of feeding rabbits. However, you may not be able to get hold of the particular food that your rabbit's breeder uses, or you may have purchased your rabbit from a pet shop. In this case, you will need to find a suitable food on your own.

There are two main types of rabbit foods: pellets and mixes. In America rabbits are generally fed on pellets, which contain all that a rabbit needs, but in Britain a good-quality rabbit mix seems to be favoured. The advantage of feeding a rabbit mix is that the mix contains more variety, and even a fussy eater will feed happily. A good-quality rabbit mix usually contains oats, barley, pellets, and flakes of dried peas and maize. Some mixes are molassed, which means that they are coated in sweet-smelling molasses. This sort of rabbit mix has a sticky texture, and is usually very popular with rabbits. Rabbit mixes that should be avoided include those containing coloured biscuits (rabbits do not usually eat these, and anything coloured should always be avoided), and mixes that do not contain an equal mix of the different ingredients. Certain newer rabbit mixes contain pieces of finely-chopped hay, as a way to feed the rabbit hay without having to purchase it separately. Some rabbits probably like this, but in my own experience, I have found that most rabbits will not eat any hay included in a mix – they prefer to be fed hay in the normal way.

HAY

Hay is essential to provide the rabbit with roughage in its diet, and should always be available. Make sure that the hay you feed is sweet-smelling. It must not be dusty, wet or mouldy. If you have to switch from one type of hay to another – especially if you have been feeding your rabbit on old stored hay, and then buy in new green hay – you must make the change gradually in order to avoid digestive upset. Care should always be taken when feeding green hay if the rabbit is not used to it.

Good-quality hay can be purchased from all pet shops, packed in plastic bags for convenience. For the rabbit owner with several rabbits it may be worth finding someone who can supply hay in bales, as this will work out considerably cheaper. A farm or a riding stables may allow you to buy hay by the bale, or you can contact a hay and straw merchant in your neighbourhood.

WATER

Water must always be available. As mentioned earlier, rabbits do drink quite a lot. In extreme weather, such as very hot summers or very cold winters, the water may have to be changed twice daily, instead of the normal once a day change. Rabbits will not drink water that has been allowed to warm up in the sun, so the water will have to be changed to a cold, fresh supply regularly. Likewise, in the winter, the rabbit's water may become too cold for it to drink or the water in the drinking bottle may even freeze and turn to ice. A rabbit that does not drink properly will soon dehydrate, and this will mean that it cannot withstand the cold. It is therefore important to check the rabbit's drinking water regularly in cold weather and change it for fresh, preferably lukewarm, water when necessary.

GREEN FOOD
To feed or not to feed green food is the next consideration. Many people have an image of the rabbit as a carrot-crunching, lettuce-eating animal. In fact, nothing could be further from the truth. To make sure that your rabbit stays healthy, it is wiser *not* to feed any green food at all. Most rabbits have such delicate stomachs that they will not tolerate any so-called 'wet' foods at all, and the likelihood is that diarrhoea will result. A rabbit will live perfectly happily on a good rabbit mix (or pellets), hay and water – nothing else is necessary. If you want to try introducing new food to your rabbit's diet, do so with great care. Try a small amount to start with, and wait to see how your rabbit reacts.

Never feed very wet vegetables such as lettuce, cucumber or tomatoes, as this type is the most likely to cause the rabbit stomach upsets. Stick to carrots, turnips, cabbage, and perhaps a small piece of apple now and then. Raw potatoes are usually also appreciated, as well as potato peelings.

BRAN MASH
A mash made of bran will benefit the rabbit at times, such as when a doe is nursing a litter, or when a rabbit is living outside in cold weather. Just mix bran with a small quantity of water (cold in the summer, warm in the winter) and feed it to the rabbit in a bowl.

QUANTITY
Normally, a rabbit will be quite happy if it is fed once a day. The time of day you choose does not really matter, as long as it is approximately the same time every day, as rabbits like their routines. Nursing does and youngsters may need feeding twice a day. A rabbit is considered full grown at five months, and from then onwards it will only need one meal a day. The amount you feed really depends on the size of the rabbit, and your rabbit's breeder is probably the best person to advise. If your rabbit appears to be very hungry, increase the daily amount of food. If the rabbit starts to become fat, reduce the amount. More often than not, it is a case of using some common sense.

GENERAL CARE
Rabbits are fairly easy to care for, and do not need to take up vast amounts of time. How much time you spend on your pet rabbit depends on the breed (as a longhaired rabbit will naturally require more grooming) and how tame you want your pet to be. Needless to say, the more time you spend with your rabbit, the tamer it will become.

CLEANING THE HUTCH
One of your most important tasks is to keep your rabbit's hutch clean. A dirty hutch

Longhaired breeds, like this sooty-fawn Cashmere Lop, need weekly grooming sessions.

When you are taming your rabbit, place it on a table and stroke it gently.

Grooming a longhaired rabbit:

When combing through the back and sides, place the rabbit on a non-slip mat on a table.

When grooming the areas underneath, sit down with the rabbit laid on its back, on your lap.

can lead to all sorts of problems. It will smell; in warm weather it will attract flies and maggots; and in the winter bedding can actually freeze if it is soaking wet. Regardless of the temperature, rabbits can catch diseases such as coccidiosis and vent disease (also known as hutch burn) from a dirty hutch.

There is no strict rule as to how often a rabbit hutch should be cleaned out. It all depends on the size of the rabbit, the size of the hutch, and how naturally clean the rabbit is. Obviously, a small rabbit in a large hutch will not need cleaning out as frequently as a larger rabbit in the same size hutch. Once again, it is important to apply common sense and judge whether the hutch needs cleaning out or not. Some rabbits are extremely clean, and will use one or two corners of their hutch as a special toilet area. In the case of rabbits like this, it is often only necessary to clean out the toilet corners frequently, whereas the rest of the hutch can be left for perhaps three weeks. Other rabbits will use the whole area of the hutch as a toilet, and then the whole hutch will need to be cleaned out as soon as it appears to be getting dirty.

When you are cleaning out the hutch, it is advisable to put your rabbit in a travelling box or an indoor cage. The easiest way to clean out a rabbit hutch is to start by using a dustpan to shovel all the soiled bedding up, and a brush to sweep everything up from the hutch floor. I find a paint-scraper is useful for removing any tough dirt. When the hutch has been thoroughly swept out, you can then fill it up with new bedding. Every six months or so, the hutch will benefit from being disinfected with some non-toxic liquid, and this should also always be done if a different rabbit is to move into the hutch, especially if the former occupant has died.

GROOMING

The safest way to handle your rabbit when it needs grooming is to place it on a table on a non-slip rubber mat (such as the type used in cars) so that your rabbit's feet will not slip and it will feel secure. When you are grooming the area on the rabbit's stomach and legs, you should sit down and hold the rabbit in your lap, laying it on its back.

SHORTHAIRED RABBITS
Whether or not a rabbit needs grooming will depend on the breed of rabbit, and whether the rabbit is in moult (shedding) or not. A shorthaired rabbit will not need regular grooming, as the coat will not mat. However, when it is in heavy moult (which usually happens once or twice a year, normally in the spring and autumn) you can help the rabbit to remove the old dead coat by grooming it with a fine metal comb or a slicker brush. If you use a slicker brush, take care not to scratch the rabbit's skin, as the metal bristles of the brush are very sharp. A rabbit that is in very heavy moult can sometimes benefit from having fur plucked out from its body by hand. Only do this if the fur is very loose – you do not want to hurt the rabbit by pulling its fur out!

LONGHAIRED RABBITS
A longhaired rabbit will need regular grooming all the year round. Most longhaired rabbits will have grown their full coat by the age of six months. From then onwards, grooming will become easier, as the very woolly baby fur can be quite difficult to

care for. There are two types of longhaired rabbits: the Angora with a very woolly fur, and the much less woolly breeds like the Cashmere Lop and the Swiss Fox. An Angora will need either very regular grooming (several times a week) to keep its fur in best condition, or it will need shearing a few times a year, like a sheep. The Angora's fur can be used for spinning wool, and this is mainly why these rabbits are kept. A show Angora will not be sheared (or clipped), so regular grooming is essential. There is no sorrier sight than an Angora with a heavily-matted coat, and I would never recommend this breed as a pet unless the owner had a real interest in grooming.

The fur of the Cashmere Lop, which is a common pet, includes a lot of heavy, non-woolly guard hairs, which gives the fur a totally different texture to that of the Angora. The fur will lie flat, and will not mat as easily. Some woolly Cashmere Lops exist, but these should be avoided in any breeding programme, as it is an undesirable fault in the breed. A Cashmere Lop with a good coat will still need regular grooming, but once a week at the most will usually be sufficient.

When grooming a longhaired rabbit, a metal comb is the best instrument to use. Start by using a wide-toothed comb, and carefully comb through all the fur, gently teasing out any knots. It is very difficult to remove large knots by combing. The best course of action is to very carefully cut off the knot, using a pair of round-tip scissors. When you have gone through the coat with a wide-toothed comb, switch to a fine-toothed comb, and go over the whole rabbit once again. The areas to pay special attention to are behind the ears, on the chest, and the stomach. Always be very careful when grooming, as a rabbit has a very sensitive skin that will easily tear if it is pulled too hard. A longhaired rabbit with a coat full of knots is a real nightmare to deal with. Neglecting your rabbit's coat will create problems for yourself, as well as causing discomfort to your rabbit. A regular routine of grooming will ensure that no problems occur.

TRIMMING CLAWS

Rabbits' claws must be trimmed on a regular basis, approximately every other month. You will need a pair of nail-clippers (see Chapter Three: Equipment), and all that is required is to gently cut the tip off each claw – not forgetting the dewclaws on the front legs. As these claws are situated an inch or so (2.5cms) up on the rabbit's leg, they will not wear down naturally, and can easily become severely overgrown if they are neglected. In extreme cases, the nails will start piercing the skin on the leg. When trimming your rabbit's claws, you should sit down and hold the rabbit firmly in your lap. Alternatively, ask someone to hold the rabbit while you cut its claws. A pale-coloured rabbit will normally have white claws. These are very easy to trim, as the pink quick is visible inside them. Cut the claw approximately half a centimetre from the quick. If you cut too close, the claw will bleed. Rabbits with dark claws present more of a problem. In this instance you cannot see the quick and so it is a case of learning how much to cut. If you are worried about this, ask an experienced breeder or vet to help you the first few times.

If you should happen to cut into the quick of a claw, do not panic. The quick will bleed profusely, but the bleeding can be stopped. It is a good idea to keep some sort of coagulant fluid in stock, which can be used to stem the blood-flow. You can usually find this at your local pharmacist in the form of a styptic pencil.

Trimming nails

Hold your rabbit firmly in your lap when undertaking this task.

Using nail-trimmers, trim the tip from each claw. This will need to be done approximately every other month.

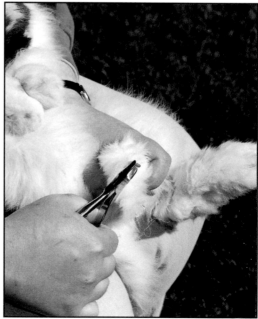

The correct way to hold a rabbit: Place one hand underneath the front legs, and support the hindquarters with your other hand.

ADDITIONAL CHECKS

Normally, a healthy rabbit will not need any other general care apart from being groomed and having its nails trimmed. However, a rabbit's teeth may sometimes become overgrown and will need special attention. (This is discussed under 'Malocclusion' in Chapter Nine: Health Care.). Likewise, a rabbit's ears do not need any attention, unless an infection is present.

A rabbit must never be bathed, as this procedure is likely to give the rabbit a serious chill and will also ruin the coat. A bath would destroy all the natural oil in a rabbit's coat, and the coat would become dry and brittle. This will mat easily, and the rabbit's skin may also itch. The only way to keep your rabbit clean is to ensure that it never gets dirty in the first place – and the key to this is to keep the rabbit's hutch clean at all times. Small stains can be wiped off with a damp cloth, but that is all that should ever be required. A healthy rabbit will lick itself several times a day, and will make sure that its coat is never dirty.

HANDLING YOUR RABBIT

In order to care for your rabbit properly, you need to learn how to handle it. A rabbit that is handled in the wrong way, or is not used to handling, will panic and can inflict nasty scratches by kicking its owner with its hindlegs. The best way to handle a new rabbit that has not yet had time to get to know its owner, is by firmly gripping the scruff, just behind the rabbit's ears, with one hand, and when lifting it up, supporting its hindquarters with the other hand. Handled in this way, the rabbit will feel secure and it is not likely to kick or struggle. Once out of the hutch, place the rabbit against your chest, with one hand supporting the hindquarters, the other across its back.

If you do not feel confident enough to carry the rabbit like this just yet, place it on a low table and gently stroke it. It helps to place a rubber mat on the table, as the rabbit's furry feet are likely to slip. A tame rabbit can be picked up by placing one hand underneath it, just behind the front legs, and the other hand once again supporting the hindquarters. If not too large, the rabbit can be carried around sitting on your arm, as long as you support it with the other arm. Under no circumstances should a rabbit be picked up by its ears, as this is very painful and will terrify the poor rabbit.

When you have just acquired a new rabbit, you should leave it to settle in for a couple of days before starting to handle it. Just feed it, and then leave it alone. After a couple of days you can start to get the rabbit used to you. The more you handle it, the tamer it will get. To gain the rabbit's confidence inside its hutch, you can start by offering it tidbits from your hand, such as a piece of plain biscuit, or a dandelion leaf. The rabbit will very soon learn that your presence means food, and it will become very excited as soon as you come near the hutch.

Once the rabbit is not worried by the presence of your hand, start to gently stroke your pet. Most rabbits love to have their foreheads scratched, and will sit perfectly still and enjoy it. Rabbits that are used to this sort of treatment will usually run up to your hand and rub their heads against it, asking for cuddles. When handling the rabbit outside the hutch, it is best to place it on a low table to start with. Make sure that the table is not too high, just in case the rabbit should panic and jump off. Once the rabbit is used to being stroked and petted on a table, you can sit it on your lap. It is important to bear in mind that rabbits do *not* like being carried around – even a very tame rabbit will protest eventually. Your rabbit will much prefer sitting on your lap for a while, or running around a room (or a very secure garden). If you get down to ground level, you will find it is easier to interact with your rabbit.

LEVELS OF RESPONSE
Rabbits are not known for being very intelligent; their intelligence cannot be compared with that of a dog or a cat. However, rabbits are among the most intelligent of small pet animals and probably rank above guinea pigs, hamsters, gerbils etc. A rabbit can be taught a few things, such as walking on a lead, jumping a fence (see Chapter 7: Showing Rabbits), and some rabbits can be taught to be clean in the house.

If you want to attempt to house-train your rabbit, you should purchase a litter tray, such as the type used for cats, and fill the tray with cat-litter. Every time the rabbit has an 'accident' in the house (while it is exercising, out of the cage), place the rabbit on the litter tray. It will also help if you pick up any solid mess and place it in the tray, as this will show the rabbit where it is meant to perform. Some rabbits will learn how to use a litter tray very quickly, others will never learn.

The one thing that *all* rabbits can be taught is to respond to their name. This can be done by using your rabbit's name on all occasions, perhaps giving a tidbit at the same time. The rabbit will soon realise the names refers to *him*, and will be quick to respond as his name is associated with pleasant experiences.

RABBIT BEHAVIOUR
Pet rabbits have got a whole range of behaviour patterns in common with their wild cousins, and if you learn to understand how a rabbit behaves, you will find it easier to care for.

CHIN-RUBBING
Your rabbit may rub its chin against objects, and possibly against its owner as well. This is the rabbit's way of telling other rabbits which objects belong to him or her. More often than not, this behaviour is seen in bucks. The rabbit has got scent glands on its chin, and by rubbing these against objects, the rabbit will deposit its own scent. In this way, other rabbits will smell this area and be able to identify the originator. Humans cannot smell this scent.

SPRAYING
The buck rabbit may spray urine over his hutch, his food bowl, and anything else within reach. Again, the rabbit is establishing ownership.

LASHING OUT WITH FORELEGS
This is an aggressive form of behaviour when the rabbit springs forward and lashes out with its forelegs. The meaning is clear: "Get out of my hutch!" This behaviour is often seen in does, especially when they are nursing.

CIRCLING
The buck rabbit keeps going around in circles, making low, purring noises. This means he is looking for a doe to mate.

With sympathetic handling, a pet rabbit will soon get used to being handled, and will enjoy the experience.

With training, a rabbit will learn to wear a harness and lead.

Rabbits soon learn to appreciate the companionship of their human owners.

ROLLING OVER
If your rabbit rolls over on its back, looking almost dead, with all four legs stretched out, there is no reason to be alarmed. The rabbit does this when it is feeling thoroughly content and happy!

BROODY DOES
This behaviour may be typified by the doe rabbit running around with tufts of hay or any other kind of bedding in her mouth, as she attempts to build a nest. This behaviour obviously also occurs in pregnant does.

HIGH-PITCHED SCREAMING
This is the rabbit's way of expressing extreme fear.

Chapter Five

RABBIT BREEDS

There are a great number of different breeds of rabbit in existence today, numbering over a hundred. Some of these make ideal pets, some are only suitable for the experienced rabbit keeper. It is not possible to list every single breed in a book of this size, so I have chosen a wide selection of the most commonly available breeds. The breeds are divided into three groups; FANCY, FUR, and REX. This is the British group system. In America and certain other countries, rabbits are divided into different groups by weight, rather than the classification of Fancy, Fur and Rex. As the Rabbit Fancy originated in Britain, I am using the British system in this context.

COLOURS
In order to understand the descriptions of the various breeds, I have listed the most common colour varieties of rabbits, and how to recognise them:

AGOUTI: This is the natural, wild, brown-grey colour, which all wild rabbits exhibit.
BLACK: As dense black as possible. The underfur is normally a blue-grey tone.
WHITE: Pure-white, with either red or blue eyes.
SOOTY FAWN: Also known as TORTOISESHELL or MADAGASCAR. This is an orange/brown top colour, with underfur of a blue tone. The sides of the rabbit, as well as the face, ears, legs, feet and tail, are shaded in a dark-grey colour.
FAWN OR YELLOW: A bright fawn colour with pale, almost white, underfur. The rabbit's stomach is white.
BLUE: An even blue-grey.
CHOCOLATE: An even, warm brown.
LILAC: Dove grey.
CHINCHILLA: This is a version of the agouti, where all-brown pigmentation has been replaced by white. The rabbit has a dark-blue under-colour, white middle-colour, and each hair is tipped with black, giving the rabbit an overall impression of silver.
SIAMESE SMOKE: Also known as SMOKE PEARL and BLUE SABLE. The colour is blue-grey, which can vary in shades, with a darker grey on the rabbit's sides, face, ears, legs, feet and tail.
SIAMESE SABLE: In some countries this is also known as BROWN SABLE. It is the brown version of Siamese smoke. The rabbit is brown, with the shade varying from light to very dark. The sides, ears, face, legs, feet and tail are very dark-grey.
SEALPOINT: Also known as SIAMESE. The colour is like the Sealpoint Siamese cat, although the eyes are not blue. The rabbit is of a beige to grey colour, with

FANCY BREEDS

*Belgian Hare:
The Greyhound
of the rabbit
world.*

*Blue Tan: This
rabbit can also
be black,
chocolate or
lilac. Its
underside is a
rich tan colour.*

*Black Himalayan:
A small, slender
rabbit that is pure
white with a
coloured face,
ears, feet and tail.
This rabbit makes
an ideal pet.*

*Harlequin:
Also known
as the
Japanese
rabbit. The
body is
striped in
two bands of
colours.*

Sealpoint Cashmere Lop: This is a new and popular breed for the pet owner. It requires regular grooming, but not the specialised attention required by a breed like the Angora.

Black Dutch: The Dutch is one of the best-known rabbit breeds, and it is highly suitable as a pet.

Blue Dutch: This breed always has a white front, with the second half of the body being coloured.

Siamese Smoke Netherland Dwarf: This is a very small, attractive rabbit, but temperament can be uncertain.

dark-grey face, ears, legs, feet and tail. The amount of dark shading can vary; some rabbits have shading confined to the lower sides of their body, others a dark-grey colour all over.

TAN PATTERN: This is a black, blue, chocolate or lilac rabbit, with a rich tan-coloured belly.

OTTER: Basically the same as tan, although the rabbit's underside is pale beige with tan coloured borders.

FOX: A coloured rabbit with a white underside.

STEEL: A much darker version of agouti.

HIMALAYAN: A pure-white rabbit with a coloured smut on the nose, and coloured ears, legs, feet and tail. The eyes are always red.

BROKEN MARKED or BUTTERFLY: A white rabbit with coloured markings; a coloured butterfly shaped smut (spot) on the nose, coloured patches around the eyes, coloured ears, a large coloured mantle on the back, and various amounts of spotting.

FANCY BREEDS

Fancy rabbits are bred for one purpose only (apart from being kept as pets), and that is to be exhibited at shows. With the exception of the Angora, whose long fur can be turned into wool, none of the Fancy breeds have ever had a practical use, such as being bred for the qualities of their meat or fur. The most common Fancy breeds are the following:

ANGORA

There is one English and one Continental version of this breed, with the English variety being slightly smaller, and mainly used as a show animal at this time. The English Angora weighs up to 6.7lb (3kgs) and comes in many different colours, including white, golden, sooty-fawn, cream, Siamese sable, blue, smoke, etc. The fur should be as long as possible and cover the whole rabbit, complete with large tufts of fur on the ears. As mentioned earlier, this breed needs constant grooming, and so does not make a suitable pet. They also need specialist housing to keep their fur from getting matted and dirty.

BELGIAN HARE

This is a fairly large breed, weighing 11 to 12lbs (5 to 5.5kgs). As the name suggests, the rabbit is similar looking to a hare, with a long body, long legs and long ears. It could perhaps be called the Greyhound of the rabbit world. The colour is usually red, with blotchy ticking across the body. This is very much a specialist breed, and a Belgian Hare may not be an ideal pet, mainly due to its large size.

DUTCH

Perhaps the best-known of all rabbit breeds, a Dutch rabbit is a white and coloured animal. The head and ears are coloured, with a white blaze in the middle. The front part of the body is white, with the second half of the body being coloured. Approximately half of the hind feet are white, with the rest being coloured. The Dutch is a fairly small rabbit, with a weight of up to 5lbs (2.3kgs). It comes in several different colours, such as black, blue, chocolate, yellow and tortoiseshell. Breeders are working on developing further colours. The Dutch makes an ideal pet.

ENGLISH
Another very well-known breed, in some countries this breed is known as the English Spot. This is a white rabbit with coloured spots, coloured ears, colour around the eyes, and a so-called coloured smut on the nose. All along the spine there is an unbroken line of colour. The English comes in black, blue, tortoiseshell, chocolate and grey. It weighs 6 to 8lbs (2.7 to 3.6kgs), and makes a very good pet.

FLEMISH GIANT
This truly is a giant breed, with the minimum weight being 11lbs (5kgs). The colour is steel-grey. Due to its size, this rabbit is perhaps not very suitable as a pet, although it is often very good-natured.

HARLEQUIN
In some countries this breed is known as the Japanese rabbit. This is a very striking rabbit, coloured in black and golden-orange. One side of the head should be black, the other orange, and the body is striped in bands of the two colours. There is a very similar variety, known as the Magpie, which is black and white. The Harlequin weighs 6 to 8lbs (2.7 to 3.6kgs) and will make a good pet.

HIMALAYAN
A fairly small and slender rabbit that is long in the body. This breed is pure-white with red eyes. It has a coloured face, ears, feet and tail, which can be black, blue, chocolate or lilac. It weighs approximately 4.5lbs (2kgs). The Himalayan is a very good-natured rabbit, of a good size, who will make an ideal pet.

DWARF LOP
In America, this breed is known as the Holland Lop. This is a very popular breed with fanciers and pet-keepers alike. The rabbit is small and compact, with floppy lop ears. The weight is up to 5.2lb (2.4kgs), although in many countries it is considerably smaller. The Dwarf Lop comes in a great variety of colours, such as white, black, blue, agouti (the 'wild' pattern), chinchilla, broken, Siamese, sable, smoke, sealpoint, fawn, sooty-fawn, etc. It makes a very good pet.

CASHMERE LOP
A fairly new and very popular breed. This is a longhaired version of the Dwarf Lop. The fur is dense and lies flat. Although the breed does require grooming, it is not as demanding as the Angora, and will make a good pet for anybody who is prepared to spend some time grooming it.

ENGLISH LOP
This is the original Lop breed and one of the very first Fancy breeds to be developed. The rabbit is longer and of a more slender build than its other Lop cousins, and has incredibly long ears. The weight is around 11 to 12lbs (5 to 5.5kgs). The ears, measured from the tip of one ear to the tip of the other, can be as much as 28ins (70cms) long. Needless to say, these extremely long ears can be very delicate, and the English Lop will need a very large hutch, to avoid treading on

Red-eyed White Netherland Dwarf: Another of the many colours of this small-eared breed.

Sooty-fawn English Lop: One of the first fancy breeds to be developed.

English: Also known as the English Spot.

Silver Grey: The silver hairs covering the body give a sparkling appearance.

FUR BREEDS
Originally bred for their fur, these rabbits are bigger and heavier than Fancy breeds.

Blanc de Hotot: This distinctive-looking rabbit is still quite rare.

Chinchilla: This pretty rabbit makes a good pet.

Argente Bleu: The shading of this breed gives a silvery-blue effect. The average weight is around 8lbs (3.6kgs).

Black Silver Fox: This rabbit can also be blue, chocolate or lilac. White hairs usually extend up the sides and back of the rabbit.

its own ears. It is a friendly rabbit, but perhaps best left to the experienced rabbit keeper. Many colours exist, including black, fawn, sooty-fawn and agouti.

FRENCH LOP
The giant of the Lop breeds. A very heavy and cobby rabbit, with ears of a more moderate length than the English Lop. The French Lop should weigh at least 10lbs (4.5kgs) and often weighs more. It comes in colours such as agouti, black, broken marked, chinchilla and sooty-fawn. The French Lop does not make a suitable pet. Its very large size makes housing difficult, and it can be very awkward to handle such a large rabbit. Although many examples of this breed are very good-natured and friendly, there is also quite a high incidence of bad-tempered French Lops.

GERMAN LOP
In America this breed is known as the Mini Lop. This Lop is between the French Lop and the Dwarf Lop in size and is similar in looks. It is available in the same colours as the French and Dwarf Lop, and weighs 6.5 to 8lbs (3 to 3.6kgs). The German Lop makes a better pet than the French Lop, but I would still say that the Dwarf Lop is the best choice of all the Lop breeds.

There are other Lop breeds, such as the Meissner Lop and the experimental (not fully recognised) Mini Lop, but these are still rare.

NETHERLAND DWARF
Next to the Dutch, probably the best known rabbit of all the breeds. The Netherland Dwarf is a very small rabbit, weighing no more than 2lbs (0.9kgs). It has very short ears – no longer than 2ins (5cms) – and it has a round body and face. This is a very attractive little rabbit that comes in a great variety of colours, such as white, black, blue, Siamese sable, smoke pearl, sealpoint, opal, tan, chinchilla, etc. The Netherland Dwarf is probably most people's ideal pet, due to its baby-like looks and its small size. However, care must be taken when choosing a pet of this breed. Some individuals can be bad-tempered, so prospective owners should try to get a chance to handle the parents of the rabbit to be able to assess the temperament. Temperament is largely inherited, and good-natured parents are likely to have good-natured babies.

POLISH
In America this breed is known as the Britannia Petite. It is the breed from which the Netherland Dwarf was originated. The name Polish does not refer to Poland, but to the rabbit's glossy coat which looks like it has been polished. Originally all Polish rabbits were white with red eyes, but these days many other colours are available, such as black, blue, Himalayan, agouti, tan, etc. The Polish is a very fine and slender rabbit, with long legs. It is of approximately the same size as the Netherland Dwarf, but the two breeds look nothing like each other, with the Polish being a far more elegant breed. Unfortunately, most Polish rabbits have a rather nasty temper and so this breed cannot be recommended as a pet for the inexperienced.

SILVER
This is a coloured rabbit, evenly covered with silver hairs all over the body, which

gives it a sparkling appearance. The Silver comes in four colours: black (known as the Silver Grey), blue (known as the Silver Blue), fawn (known as the Silver Fawn) and brown (known as the Silver Brown). This is a medium-sized rabbit of approximately 4 to 5lbs (1.8 to 2.3kgs). The Silver will make a good pet.

TAN
This is a very attractive rabbit. It has a coloured body, which can be either black, blue, chocolate or lilac, with a belly and underside of a rich, deep tan colour. The weight is approximately 4.5lbs (2kgs). The Tan makes a very good pet.

FUR BREEDS

Rabbits of Fur breeds were originally bred for a purpose, mainly for the sake of their meat and/or fur. Fur breeds are generally heavier, meatier rabbits than those of Fancy breeds. These days, rabbits of Fur breeds are mainly kept as show animals and pets, even though some, particularly the New Zealand White, are still widely used for their meat.

ALASKA
This is a shiny-black rabbit, weighing 7 to 9lbs (3.2 to 4.1kgs) – perhaps a bit too big for the average pet-keeper.

ARGENTE
This attractive breed comes in four different colours, known as the Argente de Champagne, the Argente Bleu, the Argente Brun and the Argente Creme. The rabbit has a dark undercolour, with a paler top colour of the particular shade, with the whole body evenly interspersed with darker guard hairs. This gives the rabbit the effect of being a silvery blue (in the case of the Bleu), a silvery brown (in the case of the Brun) etc. This breed weighs around 8lbs (3.6kgs), and makes a good pet.

BEVEREN
This breed is most often found in blue, but it also comes in white, black, brown and lilac. With a weight of at least 8lbs (3.6kgs), it will make a good pet if the owner has the facilities to properly house this fairly large rabbit.

BLANC DE HOTOT
A very distinctive rabbit, being pure-white with dark eyes, and black circles, almost like glasses, around the eyes. Weight is from 7.7lb to 9.9lb (3.5 to 4.5kgs). The breed is still fairly rare.

BRITISH GIANT
The Fur equivalent to the Fancy Flemish Giant. The British Giant is a very large and heavy rabbit, weighing up to 15lbs (6.8kgs) or more! The colour is usually dark steel-grey, but other colours such as white, black and blue do also exist. This rabbit may be a gentle giant, but it is far too large a breed to be kept as a pet.

CALIFORNIAN
This breed is similar to the Himalayan, but has a much rounder, meatier body. It has

New Zealand White: This rabbit weighs 9 to 12lbs (4 to 5kgs), which is probably too big for the average pet owner.

Siamese Sable: This attractive rabbit comes in a variety of different shades. It makes a good pet.

REX
Rabbits with soft, velvet-like coats – they are very friendly and make excellent pets.

Orange Rex: The standard size weighs around 6lbs (2.7 kgs).

Siamese Sable Mini Rex, weighing 3 to 4lbs (1.4 to 1.8kgs).

Ermine Rex.

Castor Rex.

Black Rex

Havana Rex

a white body with coloured face, ears, feet and tail, which can be either black, blue, chocolate or lilac. The eyes are red and the weight is 9lbs (4kgs). The Californian rabbit is usually a gentle, friendly rabbit, but may be a bit difficult to house for the average pet owner due to its size.

CHINCHILLA
A very pretty rabbit, coloured rather like the standard grey Ranch Chinchilla. The colour gives an overall silver impression. Weight 5.5 to 6.7lbs (2.5 to 3.1kgs). The Chinchilla makes a very nice pet rabbit.

CHINCHILLA GIGANTA
The giant version of the Chinchilla, weighing 9lbs or more.

FOX
A coloured rabbit of either black, blue, chocolate or lilac, with a white underside and belly. White hairs usually extend up the sdes and back of the rabbit. Weight 5.5 to 7lbs (2.5 to 3.2kgs). This breed makes a good pet.

HAVANA
A dark chocolate coloured rabbit. It weighs 5.5 to 6.5lbs (2.5 to 3kgs) and will make a good pet.

NEW ZEALAND
Fairly large and round rabbit, weighing 9 to 12lbs (4 to 5.4kgs). Colour usually white, but they also come in black, blue and red. Nice pet, but perhaps just a shade too big for the average pet owner.

SABLE
Comes as either marten sable (with a white underside) or Siamese sable (without the white underside). A rabbit of medium size, weighing 5 to 7lbs (2.3 to 3.2kgs). Comes in different shades, such as light, medium and dark. The colour is a dark sepia brown on the back, face, legs and tail, gradually becoming paler over the rest of the body. This breed makes a good pet.

SATIN
A very attractive breed with a sparkling coat. Comes in many colours, such as white (known as the ivory satin), black, blue, lilac, castor (agouti), orange, fawn, sable, smoke pearl etc. Weight 6 to 8lbs (2.7 to 3.6kgs). Makes a good pet.

SWISS FOX
A longhaired rabbit of the same coat texture as the Cashmere Lop. The rabbit has a coat of less length than the Angora, and it lies flat, unlike the fluffy Angora coat. The ears lack the tufts of fur found on the Angora. Colour is normally white, but all other colours are accepted.

   Weight 5.5 to 7lbs (2.5 to 3.2kgs). This breed will make a lovely pet for anybody interested in grooming, but who has not got the time needed to groom an Angora.

REX BREEDS

The third breed group is the one consisting of all the Rex rabbits. A Rex rabbit completely lacks guard hairs in its fur, and only has the very soft underfur. The result is a rabbit with a soft, velvet-like coat, which is very dense. The standard Rex weighs 6 to 8lbs (2.7 to 3.6kgs), with the miniature version, the Mini Rex, weighing 3 to 4lbs (1.4 to 1.8kgs). The Rex rabbits make lovely pets; they are friendly and medium in size. They come in colours such as white (known as the Ermine Rex), black, blue, lilac, Havana, smoke pearl, agouti (known as Castor Rex), sable, seal point, fox, tan, dalmatian (spotted like the dog), harlequin, tri-colour, Himalayan, etc.

Before you decide to breed from your doe, you must be confident that she is a good specimen of her breed.

Breeders strive to produce new colours and new breeds, as well as producing top-quality animals. This is a very rare rabbit – a Polish with a ̻ ·rly coat – born from a litter of normal-coated rabbits.

Chapter Six

BREEDING RABBITS

WHETHER TO BREED?
Many rabbit owners will one day consider breeding from their pet. No breeding of any animal should be undertaken lightly, and careful consideration should be given to all aspects before embarking on such a project. Ask yourself why you want to get involved with breeding rabbits:
Do you just want to breed one litter from a much-loved pet?
Do you want to breed with showing in mind?
Do you want to breed because you think you can make money out of selling rabbits?
I can understand pet owners who want to breed a litter from their treasured pet. However, if this is done, you must make sure that you really know what you are doing. Do you know how to look after the pregnant mother, and how to care for the doe and her litter? Most important of all, what will you do with the babies once they are weaned? It is no good assuming that your local pet shop will take the litter off your hands, or that you have enough friends who will want a pet rabbit. It is essential to check out potential homes before you decide to go ahead – otherwise you might find yourself stuck with five or more rabbits that you do not really want. Remember that five extra rabbits will usually mean five extra hutches!
You must also consider whether your pet doe is a good enough specimen to be bred from. It is not advisable to breed from crossbred animals. It is a sad fact that it usually is crossbred animals that end up as being unwanted. Pure bred animals have a better chance of finding a good permanent home. If you are determined to breed from a crossbred rabbit, make sure that both the doe and buck are healthy and of good temperament – and that you will be able to sell the offspring.
If you want to breed rabbits for showing, then go ahead. Just make sure that you know what it entails. Always start off with a doe that is as good as possible. You will not get very far by breeding from mediocre stock. The offspring that you do not wish to keep for yourself will obviously have to be found new homes. If you want to interest other rabbit fanciers in buying your stock, they must be of as good quality as possible. Inevitably you will get youngsters in each litter that are not quite up to show standard, and you must plan for these as well. Is there a good pet shop that is willing to take your surplus stock? If not, are you capable of humanely putting to sleep the unwanted babies?
It is by far kinder to destroy surplus babies than to advertise them as "free to good homes", and give them away to anybody who happens to come along. You brought the rabbits into this world, and so it is your responsibility to make sure, as far as possible, that the rabbits are cared for. If you cannot do this, you may have to put

them to sleep. Bear in mind that some breeds are much easier to sell as pets than others.

If you plan to breed rabbits to make money, then I suggest that you forget the whole thing. There are only two ways to make money out of rabbits. One way is to sell good, show-quality rabbits, bred from show winning stock, to other breeders and exhibitors. Achieving this standard on a regular basis takes years of dedication, and will have cost you a lot of money in the meantime. The other way is to breed rabbits for meat. This is something completely different, and is a subject that does not belong in a book about pet rabbits.

THE RIGHT AGE FOR BREEDING

Having decided that you do want to breed from your doe, you must make sure that she is of the right age. If she is too young, you will have to wait. If she is too old, your only option is to get a different doe.

Most doe rabbits can be mated for the first time at the age of around five to six months. Do not attempt to mate a doe earlier, as an immature doe may not look after her litter properly. Large breeds, such as the French Lop, need longer to mature, so with a doe of a very large breed it is better to wait until the age of nine months.

It is equally important that the doe is not too old to be used for breeding. In the case of a doe that has not previously had any litters, she must not be older than twelve months when her first litter is born. Before this age her pelvis will be soft and can stretch when giving birth. If the doe has not had a litter by twelve months, the pelvis bone will have fused in position, and cannot open properly for the doe to give birth. Once bred from, a doe can usually be used for breeding until she is three years old, sometimes four. Small breeds, such as the Netherland Dwarf and the Polish, tend to be long-lived, and does of these breeds often stay in such good condition that they can continue breeding until they are they are three or four years of age. In other breeds, does usually retire from breeding at the age of three.

Bucks who do not have to endure the strain of being pregnant, can often be used from the age of about four to five months, right up to five years. A breeding doe that is getting past her best will usually produce litters which are smaller in number, perhaps consisting of just a single baby. The babies may be of a smaller size, and the doe may even produce stillborn young. If any of these things start to happen, it is time to retire the doe.

MATING

The mating of two rabbits is not just a simple case of putting buck and doe together and waiting for nature to take its course. Whoever coined the phrase 'breeding like rabbits' was obviously not involved in breeding tame rabbits, as this can prove to be quite difficult!

The first rule regarding the mating of rabbits is that it should never, ever be done in the doe's hutch. The doe will defend her hutch from intruders, and will no doubt attack any visiting buck. The mating should be done either in the buck's hutch, or on neutral ground. The female rabbit is one of very few animals that can be mated even when she is not in heat. The act of mating will actually trigger the doe to ovulate, so a mating done at any time can be successful. This is unlike other small livestock such as guinea pigs and hamsters, which can only be mated successfully when the females are in heat. Having said that, the doe rabbit will actually come into heat approximately every seventeen to twenty-one days. She will then be willing to mate, and a mating at this time will be easier to achieve. A doe in heat will wiggle her tail when her back is touched, and she will crouch low on her forelegs with her tail stuck up into the air, ready for the buck to mate her. If you see this behaviour in your doe, try to have her mated as soon as possible.

Assuming that your doe is in heat and is willing to be mated, you can let her into the buck's hutch. Hopefully, mating will then take place fairly promptly. Certain breeds of rabbit, notably the placid Dwarf Lops and Cashmere Lops, can safely be left together overnight without supervision. But most breeds will need strict supervising while mating, to prevent the doe from turning on the buck once she has been mated.

If the doe is not in heat, particularly if she is of a very lively and perhaps bad-tempered breed, such as the Polish, or if the buck is very inexperienced, then it is up to you to hold the doe while the buck is mating her. Put one hand over the doe's neck and ears, with the other hand underneath her body, gently lifting her backside slightly upwards, so that the buck can enter her easily. Sometimes it may be necessary to try to take hold of the doe's tail to keep it out of the way. A doe who is unwilling to mate may press her tail tightly against her vagina, to make it impossible for the buck to mate her.

A mating usually starts by the buck running around the doe, softly humming, sniffing her and licking her. He will then mount the doe. A successful mating will end with the buck letting out a grunting noise, then quickly throwing himself off the doe. He will then proceed to wash himself. At this stage you can check whether the mating was done properly or not. If the buck effected a proper mating, you will be able to see that the doe's vagina is wet. Allow the buck to mate the doe at least once more. The more times he mates her, the better the chance of the doe falling pregnant. She can become pregnant after only one mating, but two or three matings are preferable. Not many bucks will mate more than four or five times, so after this the doe can be removed to her own hutch.

IS THE DOE PREGNANT?
The gestation period for a rabbit is 28-34 days, with 30-32 days being the average. It can be quite difficult to tell whether the doe is pregnant or not, as the vast majority do not actually look pregnant. An experienced breeder or vet will be able to feel the rabbit foetuses inside the doe after approximately three weeks, by carefully palpating the abdomen. This should never be attempted by a novice, as it could harm the unborn babies if it is not done correctly. Usually, your best bet is to wait thirty-four days from the day of the mating. If nothing has happened by then, the doe was not pregnant, and you will have to try again.

THE PREGNANT DOE
The first sign that the doe is actually pregnant is when you see her preparing a nest for her litter. The nest will usually be built in a corner of the rabbit's hutch, and it will consist of hay and/or straw, lined with fur which the doe will pluck from her own abdomen. The nest is very important, as any babies born or kept outside a warm nest will not survive as they will be too cold. Some does are better nest-builders than others. A really good doe will make a huge nest, and pluck so much fur from her

This broken-marked French Lop is a few days old: The fur is just beginning to grow.

A litter of French Lops in their nest-box: Rabbits are born without any fur.

The same litter of French Lops, now two weeks old.

Rabbits usually make good mothers. This Fawn Cashmere Lop is caring for her three-week-old litter.

belly – and possibly front legs as well – that she will be partially bald. This is perfectly normal, and is nothing to worry about. The fur will soon grow back.

If the doe is not a very good nest-builder, you might have to help her by adding soft hay to the nest. Some does tend to pluck their fur, only to leave it scattered around the hutch. If this happens, you should collect all the fur and place it in the nest. Some breeders like to give their nursing doe a so-called nest box. This is a box made of wood, just large enough for the doe to sit in. A nest box has both pros and cons. The advantage is that it can easily be removed from the hutch so that the litter can be inspected. The babies are also more likely to stay in one place. The disadvantage is that any baby that happens to fall out of the nest box (which occasionally may happen if a hungry baby holds on to the doe's teats as she jumps out of the nest box) will not be picked up by the doe and put back into the nest. As the nest is inside a box, the baby will not be able to get back in on its own, and it will die if it is not found in time by the breeder.

Most does will start nesting a couple of days before the litter is due to be born. Some will leave it as late as a few hours before giving birth. If the doe starts nesting two to three weeks after mating, you can usually assume that she is not pregnant. False or phantom pregnancies are very common in rabbits. The doe will believe that she is pregnant – sometimes when she has not even been mated – and she will build a nest and will generally behave as though she were pregnant.

PREPARING FOR THE BIRTH

As it is not always possible to know for certain whether or not the doe is pregnant, it is best to assume that she is. Around twenty-seven days after the mating, the doe's hutch should be cleaned out, and filled with plenty of wood shavings and/or straw, plus hay. It is vital that the doe has a good supply of nesting material. Make sure that food and water are available at all times, as a thirsty or hungry doe may occasionally kill and eat her babies after the birth.

THE BIRTH

Most domestic rabbits will give birth during the night or early morning when no-one is around. It is very rare to see any signs of the birth, such as blood. The hutch will probably look perfectly clean. The only way to be sure that the doe has given birth or not is to inspect the nest. Carefully feel inside the nest to see if there are any babies. Keep a close eye on the doe, or remove her from the hutch, as she may attack any intruder after the litter has been born. She will usually cover her litter so well that it is impossible to see whether the nest is full or empty, without feeling.

If you can feel babies in the nest, leave well alone for the first couple of days. Even very tame rabbits can be extremely sensitive, and you must always remember that a nursing doe that is disturbed may attack and kill her babies in a sort of misguided attempt to protect them. Therefore, it is important to make sure that the doe has as much peace and quiet as possible during the first few days. Always try to plan matings so that the litter will not arrive at a very busy time. Some does will kill their babies if they are disturbed, others will scatter the nest and babies in all directions, which is just as bad, as the babies will die from the cold if they are not discovered very soon.

INSPECTING THE LITTER

Approximately three days after the birth, you should try to inspect the litter. Always remove the doe from the hutch first, to cause her as little distress as possible. Before attempting to handle the babies, it is a good idea to rub your hands in some soiled bedding from the hutch, as this will mask your scent. Gently part the nest, and look at the babies inside. Quite commonly, there will be one or two dead babies which must be removed. Dead babies are usually found buried right at the bottom of the nest. Check that the rest of the litter looks healthy.

You may well find that one or two babies are much smaller than their littermates, perhaps only a third of the size of their siblings. Such babies are termed runts, and they will usually die as they are not strong enough to compete for the food with their larger littermates. You should now decide whether to remove such babies and have them put to sleep (culled, as it is generally known) by using chloroform, or by a sharp blow to the head – or whether you prefer to leave them with their mother, where they will either die naturally, or may sometimes survive.

My personal experience is that such babies very seldom survive. Culling is always an emotive issue and is the subject of much discussion. In most cases, it is only the runts that are culled. However, it may also be necessary in order to reduce the size of a very large litter if the doe is failing to cope. In this instance, it may also be needed if it is going to be difficult to home a very large litter. Selection should be made according to size, with the smallest and weakest babies being culled. If there is no difference in size, it can be a question of selection due to the markings, as in the case of Dutch and English rabbits.

Normal litter size for a small doe, such as a Netherland Dwarf or a Polish, is two to four babies, although it can vary from one to six. Does of these small breeds can usually cope well with up to six babies. Slightly larger breeds, such as the Dwarf Lop, will normally have litters consisting of three to five babies, although numbers as high as nine can occur. Giant breeds usually have very large litters, with anything from five to twelve being quite common.

CARING FOR THE LITTER

The rabbit babies will remain in their nest for ten to fourteen days. During this time you can inspect them every day if the doe does not get distressed. The hutch must not be cleaned out completely for at least three weeks, as the doe will be very distressed if her nest is disturbed. If the hutch gets badly soiled, try to remove the soiled areas only, and replace with clean bedding.

The doe will need more food than normal as long as she is suckling. Feeding twice a day instead of the usual one meal is a good idea, and supplements such as a bran mash every day will help to keep her milk supply going. You are not likely to see the doe suckling her litter. This is no cause for concern, as rabbits only suckle their young a couple of times during a twenty-four hour period, and most often this will be at night. If the babies are thriving, they are obviously getting enough to eat.

The babies will start to leave the nest once their eyes have opened, which normally occurs at any time from ten to fourteen days of age. They will now start to explore their surroundings and you should start to handle them regularly, to get them used to people. Once the babies have left the nest, the family will need a very large supply of food, as the babies will now start to eat the same food as the mother. Make sure that you use a bowl which the babies can easily reach into.

Rabbit babies are born naked, but they usually have a hint of pigmentation at birth. This means that you will be able to distinguish between pale and dark-coloured animals immediately after birth. After a day or two, more pigmentation will appear and it will be easy to tell if one particular baby is self-coloured or broken marked. After about a week the babies are fully covered with fur. At this stage the fur will not have the correct shade of colour, as it is very short. For example, an agouti coloured rabbit looks more black than brown. At around the age of two weeks it should be fully possible to tell what colours the babies are.

How long the babies stay with their mother will depend on the mother. Most does will let the babies know, in no uncertain terms, when they have had enough of them. The doe will start to chase them away and nip them if they come too close. In certain breeds, such as the Polish, this often occurs as early as four weeks of age. Other breeds may tolerate their offspring for a further three weeks. In any case, rabbit babies are best left with their mother until they are at least five, and preferably six, weeks of age. It is a good idea to remove all the litter from the mother at the same time, and keep them together in a separate hutch, before selling them. In this way, the change from living with the mother to living on their own will be a gradual one

Once the litter has been removed, the doe should be allowed some time to rest before being mated again. The length of time she needs to recover will depend on what condition she is in. If she is thin, with hardly any fur on her belly, she will need a much longer period of time than if she remained in good condition with little or no weight loss, and still with fur on her belly. Personally, I would not like to breed from a doe more than three times a year, but opinions on this will always vary among breeders.

Chapter Seven

SHOWING RABBITS

For the rabbit owner who has started to take an interest in breeding, showing is very often the next logical progression. Rabbit shows have been held since the early 19th century in Britain, and nowadays shows are staged more or less every weekend of the year. In America, most rabbit shows are held during the spring and the autumn, as the summer is often too hot for these events to take place. Showing rabbits is a hobby, just like showing dogs or any other animal. It will enable you to make new friends with the same interest as you. If you want to breed pure bred rabbits, then showing is more or less a must. It is only by showing your rabbits that you can find out what their good and bad points are, and it will tell you a lot about what you need to concentrate on in your breeding programme. There is a wealth of knowledge among the exhibitors and judges at rabbit shows, and as a regular exhibitor you will learn a great deal about rabbits and rabbit keeping.

HOW TO START SHOWING
The procedures that are adopted at rabbit shows will vary from country to country. For details of shows and showing, contact your country's governing body. In Britain, the British Rabbit Council (BRC) will be able to give you details of shows coming up in your area, and these will also be advertised in the official magazine of the BRC, *Fur and Feather*. In America, the American Rabbit Breeders' Association will supply all the relevant information.

The best way of getting involved in the show scene is to start by visiting a rabbit show, as a spectator only. You can then watch the procedures, and you will, no doubt, find somebody who is willing to give you more information, such as the show secretary or exhibitors. The first thing that you need to ascertain is that your rabbit is eligible to be exhibited. Your rabbit must be pure bred, and in Britain it must be rung with an official BRC ring around one of its hindlegs. This is a lightweight metal ring that shows the rabbit's year of birth, a letter which relates to the size of the ring, and the rabbit's registration number. The ring is put on by the breeder of the rabbit, when the rabbit is three to nine weeks old. It is not possible to fit a ring on to an adult rabbit. In many other countries, including America, rabbits are tattooed with a number inside one ear, instead of being rung. American pure bred rabbits are also issued with a pedigree – this is not the case in the UK. You must also ensure that the rabbit is registered in your name.

TYPES OF SHOW
There are different grades of shows, and I would advise anybody that is planning to

enter their very first rabbit show to enter one of the smaller, lower-graded shows. Competition at the large, national shows is very hard, and you may prefer to enter your rabbit at a small show as a start, since you will not yet know how good your rabbit is. It can be very disheartening to go straight for a large Championship show, where Champions will compete, and your rabbit may be one of several unplaced in its class. At a smaller show, there may be only two or three entries in your rabbit's breed class, and you may well come home with a prize card.

BRC shows are star-rated. There are 1, 2, 3, 4 and 5-star shows. 1-star shows are the smallest of shows, with 5-star shows being the very biggest and most prestigious. Most local rabbit clubs tend to run 1- or 2-star shows and these are a very good place to start off. In America, rabbit shows are not graded.

Having found the show of your choice, you will need to make your entry. In Britain rabbits are usually entered into several classes, depending on breed, colour and age, and the breeds are divided into the three groups, Fancy, Fur and Rex. In the US, rabbits are entered in one class only.

PREPARING YOUR RABBIT FOR THE SHOW

How much show preparation your rabbit will need depends on the breed and colour of the rabbit. Many rabbits will need hardly any preparations at all, others will need quite a lot. Any longhaired breed will obviously need careful grooming before the show. Make sure that the fur is completely free of knots. Shorthaired breeds will not usually need grooming, other than a quick wipe down with your hands to make the fur shine. If you are showing a white rabbit, make sure that it is as clean as possible, without any stains. The only way to ensure this is to keep the rabbit's hutch as clean as possible so that the white fur will not get stained. Smaller stains can be wiped away with a damp cloth, but you must never bathe a rabbit. Bathing will more than likely give the rabbit a cold, and it will to a certain extent ruin the coat. Therefore, the only way is to ensure that the rabbit never gets dirty in the first place! A self-coloured black rabbit may have some white hairs in its coat. These can be carefully plucked out before the show, using a pair of tweezers.

An adult rabbit should have its claws trimmed short before the show. Do not trim the claws of a rabbit if it is under five months of age. Some judges believe that only adult rabbits need their claws trimmed, and may not believe that a rabbit with trimmed claws is actually not yet adult.

Other than this, the only preparation your rabbit will need is to be used to being handled. Certain breeds, such as the Polish and the Belgian Hare, will also need to be taught the correct posture to sit in, once at the judging table. Ask more experienced exhibitors for advice on this.

THE DAY OF THE SHOW

The best way to transport your rabbit to the show is in a proper rabbit travelling box or in a cat carrier (See Chapter Three: Equipment). Try to arrive at the show at least half an hour before judging is due to commence. You will need this time to settle your rabbit into its show pen, and for some final grooming.

Different shows tend to have different procedures, but usually the first thing that you will do upon arrival at the show hall is to report to the show secretary that you have arrived and to pay your entry fees. You will then be given your rabbit's pen number, and can go off to find the pen allocated to you. The pen will probably be furnished with wood shavings, so you might want to add some hay for comfort, and a water bottle. Once you have settled your rabbit into its pen, all you have to do is wait. When the judging starts, stewards will carry the rabbits to and from the judging table. Exhibitors will not be allowed inside the immediate judging area, but you can watch from a distance to get an idea of what is going on.

THE JUDGING PROCEDURE
There are usually at least two judges at each show, and bigger shows will naturally have a greater number of judges. The judge will examine each rabbit in turn, and make notes on its good and bad points. Each breed has a written Breed Standard, which has been drawn up by specialists in the breed. The Breed Standard may vary from country to country, and in the US it may even vary from state to state. However, the role of the judge is the same, and that is to assess each rabbit by how closely it conforms to the Breed Standard in use, and then to compare the rabbits entered against each other.

Each Breed Standard states exactly what each breed of rabbit should look like: how big the rabbit should be, if it should be cobby or slender, what shape the head should be, how long or short the coat should be, as well a description of what the perfect colour should look like. For example, both a Netherland Dwarf and a Polish rabbit should be of approximately the same size, with large, round eyes, and small ears held erect, and close together. But where the Netherland Dwarf is short and cobby with a round, broad head, the Polish is of a more slender build with a longer face. A Polish or Netherland Dwarf with over-large ears will be penalised, but an English Lop should have ears that are as long as possible.

THE BRITISH SYSTEM
In Britain each section of Fancy, Fur and Rex is judged separately, class by class. The judge will bring a complete class on to the judging table at once, so that he or she can easily compare the rabbits. There will be one steward looking after each rabbit, so that no fights will break out, even though the rabbits will be placed next to each other.

The judge will pick the winner, a second and a third, and then the winning rabbits of a particular breed will compete for the Challenge Certificates (CCs) and Best of Breed (BOB). Eventually, all BOB winning Fancy rabbits will compete against each other to select an overall Best Fancy. The same thing will happen in the Fur and Rex sections. At the end of the day there will be one Best Fancy winner, one Best Fur winner, and one Best Rex winner. Competition may finish here, or the three main winners may compete against each other for an overall Best in Show. Any cards and/or rosettes won will be placed on the rabbit pens, for everyone to see. No written report will be given on the day. A judge's report on all the winners will appear in a later edition of *Fur & Feather*.

If you are lucky enough to have a rabbit that has won a Challenge Certificate, you will have to look after the award carefully as CCs will count towards awards such as the BRC Silver Star Diploma and Championship Diploma. Rules can be obtained from the BRC.

THE AMERICAN SYSTEM
In America, you will be more likely to enter your rabbit on the day of the show. On

Each rabbit is examined individually by the judge. Here he is assessing a Black Rex.

Each breed may be weighed to ensure that it is within the limits stipulated by the breed standard.

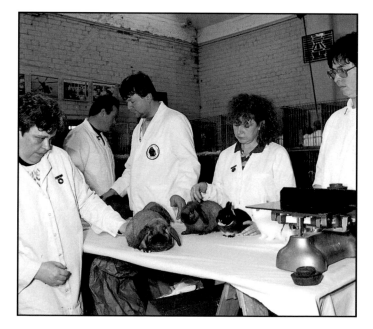

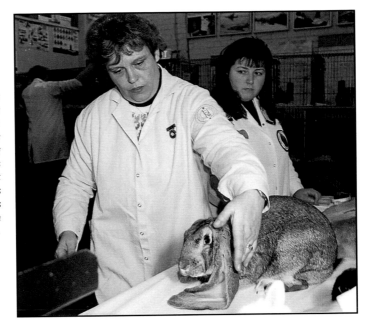

The judge must be familiar with the distinguishing characteristics of the different breeds. This judge is examining an English Lop.

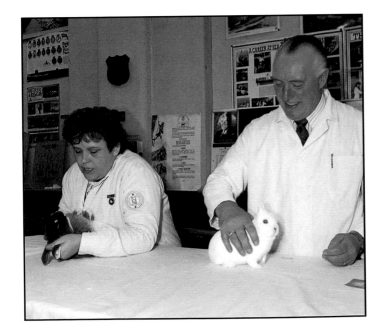

At the end of the show, the judges may meet together and select the overall Best in Show exhibit.

arrival at the show, you will be asked to fill out an entry form for your rabbit stating breed, colour, sex, age, etc. Judging is conducted in a similar way to rabbit judging in Britain, although you will be required to carry your rabbit to the judging table yourself, rather than a steward doing the task.

After the judging has been completed, each exhibit will be issued a signed score card, which will state how many points (out of a given maximum) your rabbit has gained, both in each separate section, such as colour, ears, etc., and an overall total is added. The card will also state how many rabbits were entered in the class, and where your rabbit was placed. Full show rules can be obtained from the American Rabbit Breeders' Association.

SHOW JUMPING

Rabbit show jumping is an increasingly popular sport in Scandinavia, with both children and adults taking part. To date, the sport does not exist in countries outside Scandinavia, but it is only a matter of time before it is adopted elsewhere.

THE ORIGINS

Rabbit show jumping originated in Sweden during the early 1980s. Ironically, it all came about as a direct result of what some British children had been doing! The television programme, *That's Life*, once screened a fun item about some children that had taught their pet rabbits to jump fences, like a miniature version of 'real' show jumping with horses. This clip was eventually shown as part of a Swedish children's television programme, and it inspired a number of children to try this game out with their own pet rabbits. They were so successful that magazine articles were written about them, and when the number of 'rabbit jumpers' (as they call themselves) had grown large enough, rabbit show jumping was introduced as an attraction at rabbit shows and other pet shows.

More and more people started to get interested; rules for the competition were formally laid down, and clubs especially for this new sport were formed. The first-ever Swedish Championship in rabbit show jumping took place in 1987, with sixty rabbits competing. The following year the number had grown to one hundred and twenty, and today there are two thousand active rabbit jumpers all over Sweden, with as many as fifty clubs catering for their sport. The sport has also gained popularity in Norway and Denmark.

To start with, the sport was confined exclusively to children, but increasingly, adults are becoming involved. It is a highly popular spectator sport, and it has received a lot of coverage in the media. Organisers of large shows and exhibitions often feature rabbit show jumping as a major attraction.

IS IT CRUEL?

The practice of rabbit show jumping is definitely not cruel. The rabbits jump because they like it, and have been trained to do so using lots of praise and rewards. Any handler that is seen to push, jerk or kick his or her rabbit at a show jumping event will immediately be disqualified. It is also true to say that it is almost impossible to train a rabbit as a show jumper using force. The rabbits co-operate because they enjoy jumping.

The pro-jumpers of Sweden put forward the opinion that show jumping rabbits have a healthier and more interesting life than other rabbits, and I am inclined to agree. A rabbit that regularly jumps at shows, or simply for fun, will be a well-looked-after, happy rabbit. The rabbit will be very fit due to all the exercise, and it must be kept in this tip-top condition to be able to jump. The rabbit will certainly enjoy a more varied and stimulating life, rather than being confined to a hutch for long periods like most pet and show rabbits. The natural way for a rabbit to move is by jumping, so you are not teaching your rabbit anything that is unnatural. You are just expanding on the abilities that are already there.

TEACHING YOUR RABBIT TO JUMP

Any breed of rabbit will make a suitable show jumping prospect, apart from possibly Angoras, whose long fur may get in the way. Dwarf Lops are very popular jumpers in Sweden as they are so good-natured. Any rabbit that is being trained to jump must be very tame and used to being handled on a regular basis.

The best age to start training is around four months when the rabbit is neither too young nor too old to learn. Do not attempt to teach an older rabbit how to jump fences, as it can be a frightening experience for a rabbit which has, perhaps for years, been kept in a hutch and only handled once or twice a week. Both sexes will make equally good show jumpers, and the average rabbit will normally be able to clear fences of up to 3ft (90cms), although the heights will need to be much lower in the beginning.

The first step in show jumping training is to get your rabbit used to wearing a harness and lead – the type designed for cats is the most suitable. You can, of course, allow your rabbit to jump freely indoors, but outside a harness and lead is essential to ensure that your rabbit cannot escape.

You do not need to construct special fences for your rabbit to start with. Almost anything will do – some books, an empty shoebox, a pair of shoes – just use your imagination! If you find that your rabbit likes show jumping, then perhaps you can use some wood to make miniature versions of horse show jumping fences.

To teach your rabbit to jump, the most important attribute that you will need is *patience*. Some rabbits will learn quickly, other slowly, some will not learn at all. Do not persevere if your rabbit is not enjoying itself; the key word here is that both you and your pet should have *fun*.

The first stage is to allow your rabbit to get acquainted with the fence/obstacle by sniffing at it. Then place the rabbit in front of the fence, say the word "Jump", and gently push its bottom. Most rabbits will soon get the idea. Slow learners will benefit from being gently lifted over the fence to start with. Once your rabbit has jumped, give lots of praise, and perhaps a tidbit as a reward. Then all you have to do is to keep on practising!

Chapter Eight

HEALTH CARE

A pet rabbit that is properly looked after will usually live for around five years. The dwarf breeds, such as the Netherland Dwarf and the Polish, are very hardy little rabbits that quite commonly reach ages of seven years or older. There have even been instances of dwarf rabbits living for thirteen years! However, this is very rare, and five years should be seen as the average.

The biggest threats to a rabbit's health are incorrect diet and dirty living quarters. Many of the common rabbit diseases can be avoided, if the rabbit is fed on a good diet, and lives in a hutch that is kept clean. Needless to say, there are also certain viruses that can attack rabbits, but these can affect any rabbit, no matter how well looked after it is.

I have compiled a guide to the most common diseases found in pet rabbits; how to spot them and treat them. It is only a general guide. If you are ever unsure about your rabbit's health, do not hesitate to contact a veterinarian.

COCCIDIOSIS
Symptoms: Varied. Commonly the rabbit suffers from acute, very severe diarrhoea, but in less acute cases this may not be so. The rabbit loses weight, the fur loses its shine, and the rabbit develops a so-called pot-belly – a distended stomach. Coccidiosis is a common cause of death in rabbits, especially youngsters.
Cause: Coccidiosis is caused by a parasite, which is quite commonly present in rabbit hutches. The eggs of the parasite (which are known as oocysts) are passed out with the faeces of an infected animal. If the right conditions are present, such as warm and humid weather, the eggs will become infected. If they are later eaten by the rabbit, they will develop into parasites that attack the rabbit's intestine.
Treatment: The most important way to control Coccidiosis, is to make sure that the rabbit's hutch is kept clean, especially during hot weather. If it is cleaned out often enough, the eggs will never have a chance to become infected, and so the rabbit is at no risk.

More often than not, Coccidiosis is the result of the rabbit having been kept in a very dirty hutch. There used to be special rabbit food available, which contained anti-Coccidiosis medication. Unfortunately, such feeds are now banned by law in Britain. There is medication available that can be added to the rabbit's drinking water as a way of preventing the disease. Ask your vet for advice. The only really effective way of treating Coccidiosis is to prevent it from occurring.

Once a rabbit is ill with Coccidiosis, there is very little chance of it surviving. Many rabbits will die of acute diarrhoea, something that often is referred to as 'scouring' by rabbit fanciers. The rabbit owner may never realise the real cause of the rabbit's death. Other rabbits will survive after treatment from a vet. However, such rabbits very rarely regain their original condition, and they will probably be useless for showing or breeding. In most cases rabbits that have suffered from Coccidiosis will die within a year or so. My personal experience is that it is kinder to the rabbit to have it put to sleep than to try to cure it of Coccidiosis.

WORMS
Symptoms: Pot-belly, poor coat, poor growth in youngsters. Sometimes worms can actually be seen around the rabbit's tail.
Cause: Worms are fairly rare in rabbits, but they can occur. Roundworms are the most common type, but tapeworm can also occur. An infected rabbit may have got worms by eating grass containing eggs, or a youngster may have caught it from its mother.
Treatment: Worming with a mild liquid wormer, such as used for kittens. Ask your vet for advice on dosage. Wormers bought from a veterinary surgery are usually safer and more effective than those bought over the counter.

EXTERNAL PARASITES
Symptoms: Small parasites, such as mites, can actually be seen on the rabbit's fur, usually around the face and neck. The rabbit may be seen to be scratching at its fur.
Cause: Mites are usually brought in via infested hay, or from another infested animal.
Treatment: As mentioned before, never bath a rabbit. The rabbit can be sprayed with an insecticidal spray, or treated orally or by injection with parasite cures. Ask your vet for advice. A so-called 'fly-block' can be useful if the rabbit is kept in a shed or indoors. Place the fly-block near the rabbit's hutch, but not directly on top of it. A fly-block will kill off most parasites and flies, and it is usually effective for three months. It is available from any retailer of pest control products.

RINGWORM
Symptom: Lots of white dandruff, usually found on the rabbit's neck and back. Fur loss.
Cause: A fungus. Ringworm is very infectious, and can be transferred to and from other animals, including humans. In humans, the symptoms are circular red patches on the skin, which will itch. (Hence the name ringworm.)
Treatment: Ringworm can be very difficult to get rid of, as the spores of the fungus can be carried on the rabbit's bedding, its hutch, the owner's clothes, etc. The rabbit will need medication prescribed by a vet, and in certain cases it may even be necessary to risk bathing the rabbit in a fungicide.

ABSCESSES
Symptoms: A swelling anywhere on the rabbit's body, which can be either soft or hard to the touch.
Cause: Usually the abscess is the result of a bite, commonly from another rabbit, which has become infected. Any wounds found on a rabbit should be treated with a disinfectant immediately, to prevent abscesses from occurring.
Treatment: The abscess will have to be lanced and emptied. If it has not burst on its

own, it is advisable to ask your vet to lance it. Once the abscess has been emptied of all infected pus, it will have to be cleansed thoroughly, and the rabbit's owner must continue to squeeze out any pus that occurs in the next few days, to prevent the abscess from reappearing. In severe cases, a course of antibiotics may be needed from the vet.

VENT DISEASE
(ALSO KNOWN AS HUTCH BURN)
Symptoms: The rabbit's genitalia are sore and swollen. If the rabbit has been licking itself, there may be blisters on the mouth and around the nose as well. This condition is more common in does than in bucks.
Cause: Commonly caused by rabbits being kept in dirty hutches. The disease can also be transferred via mating. A seemingly healthy buck may be a carrier of the disease, and will pass it on to the doe when mating.
Treatment: Always make sure that the rabbit's hutch is clean. This is especially important in the case of a rabbit with vent disease. The sores will need treatment with ointment obtained from your vet. In severe cases, antibiotics may be needed.

SNUFFLES
Symptoms: This disease is every rabbit breeder's nightmare, as it is very contagious and easily spreads to all rabbits kept on the same premises. The rabbit sneezes, has a runny nose and eyes, and generally loses condition. The fur on the inside of the front legs becomes matted, as the rabbit uses these to wipe its nose.
Cause: Bacteria, usually of the Pasteurella kind. Usually passed on from one infected rabbit to another.
Treatment: Antibiotics from your vet. This disease may well be fatal, and it is vital to do whatever possible to isolate any infected rabbits from healthy ones to prevent a further spread. If you keep several rabbits, the use of a quarantine hutch – placed at least ten feet away from the other hutches – will be very useful. Isolate any rabbit that shows symptoms, and if you want to be extra careful, also isolate any rabbit that has just been brought in or has visited a show, for a few days. Rabbits can become infected even if not in direct contact, as infected droplets can be carried in the air when a rabbit sneezes.

CONSTIPATION
Symptoms: Lack of droppings in the rabbit's hutch. The rabbit becomes lethargic and has an extended belly.
Cause: Several. Lack of water. The rabbit has been eating straw.
Treatment: In mild cases, it is usually enough to feed the rabbit some green food, such as carrot or lettuce. (Lettuce should never be fed under other circumstances.) If the rabbit does not want to eat, a few drops of paraffin oil or corn oil will usually do the trick.

DIARRHOEA
(ALSO KNOWN AS SCOURS)
Symptoms: The rabbit has very loose or liquid droppings. The tail area will become wet and dirty.
Cause: Several. Stress. Change of diet. Overfeeding with green food. It could also be

Coccidiosis (see notes on this).
Treatment: Feed the rabbit on dry food only, such as a rabbit mix or pellets, and hay. Make sure that water is freely available, as a rabbit with diarrhoea may become dehydrated quickly if it does not drink enough. In severe cases, a few drops of liquid charcoal will usually help. If all this fails, see a vet.
Note: Do not confuse diarrhoea with the soft droppings that are passed by rabbits during the night. These soft droppings are perfectly normal. They contain a high amount of vitamin B, and the rabbit needs to eat them to be able to benefit from the vitamin.

BLOAT
Symptoms: The rabbit's belly becomes very distended, and it appears blown up like a balloon. The rabbit will sit huddled up in a corner of its hutch, not wishing to eat or move.
Cause: Usually overfeeding of fresh food, such as green hay or clover. Gas builds up in the rabbit's stomach.
Treatment: See a vet as soon as possible, as death will occur if this condition is not treated properly.

MALOCCLUSION
Symptoms: The rabbit's teeth grow misaligned, so that the upper and the lower teeth do not meet. As a result of this, the teeth are not worn down naturally, and will start to grow too long. Eventually the rabbit will find it impossible to eat.
Cause: This is usually an inherited condition, so affected rabbits should not be bred from.
Treatment: Clipping of the teeth will be necessary, often on a regular basis. This can be done with the use of wire-cutters – the rabbit will not have to be under anaesthetic. The experienced rabbit keeper can perform this simple operation, but if you are unsure, ask your vet to show you exactly how to do it.

MYXOMATOSIS
Symptoms: This is a virus disease which is always fatal. It is often present in wild rabbits, and was deliberately brought into the British population of wild rabbits to reduce the numbers. Affected rabbits will show swollen eyelids, with swellings at the base of the ears and around the nose, sometimes also at other parts of the body. Death usually occurs within a few days.
Cause: Infection from another rabbit. In areas where there are a lot of wild rabbits, Myxomatosis can be common.
Treatment: Affected rabbits cannot be treated. There is a vaccine available from vets, so if you live in an area with a high incidence of Myxomatosis (such as an area with a lot of wild rabbits) ask your vet for details about vaccination.

RABBIT VIRAL HAEMORRAGHIC DISEASE (RVHD)
This is the most recent – and worrying – disease to afflict rabbits. It has killed hundreds of thousands of rabbits on the Continent, and it arrived in Britain in 1992. Other countries have the use of a vaccine to prevent further outbreaks, but no such vaccine is available in the UK. However, as of mid-November 1994, the British Ministry of Agriculture, Fisheries and Food (MAFF) were considering granting a

licence under special emergency licensing regulations to one or two pharmaceutical companies that tendered to distribute the vaccine in Britain.

RVHD was first recorded in China in 1984 and the disease spread rapidly throughout Europe. RVHD is extremely infectious and is classed as a 'vector' which means that it can be carried on items such as clothing, and even on frozen dead rabbits. Indeed, the virus spread from China to Mexico via frozen rabbit carcasses exported for food sale. To date there have been no recorded domestic outbreaks in North America.

RVHD is a notifiable disease, which means that, by law, any suspected outbreak should be reported to MAFF. It first occurred in Berkshire, southern England, in April 1992 within two separate studs of Fancy rabbits. Since then, it has spread throughout the country, with 126 cases reported in a two-year period. It has moved to the wild rabbit population, but the full extent of the infection is difficult to quantify, as most infected specimens would probably die underground in their own burrows.